Better Homes and Gardens®

SHORTCUT
RECIPES

©1981 by Meredith Corporation, Des Moines, Iowa.
All Rights Reserved. Printed in the United States of America.
First Edition. Second Printing, 1981.
Library of Congress Catalog Card Number: 80-68541
ISBN: 0-696-00655-3

On the cover:
When you need a meal in minutes, prepare
Peppery Fish Stir-Fry (see recipe, page 28).

BETTER HOMES AND GARDENS® BOOKS
Editor: Gerald M. Knox
Art Director: Ernest Shelton

Food and Nutrition Editor: Doris Eby
Senior Food Editor: Sharyl Heiken
Senior Associate Food Editors: Sandra Granseth,
    Elizabeth Woolever
Associate Food Editors: Bonnie Lasater,
    Julia Martinusen, Marcia Stanley,
    Joy Taylor, Diana Tryon
Recipe Development Editor: Marion Viall
Test Kitchen Director: Sharon Stilwell
Test Kitchen Home Economists: Jean Brekke,
    Kay Cargill, Marilyn Cornelius,
    Maryellyn Krantz, Marge Steenson

Associate Art Directors: Neoma Alt West, Randall Yontz
Copy and Production Editors: David Kirchner,
    Lamont Olson, David A. Walsh
Assistant Art Director: Harijs Priekulis
Senior Graphic Designer: Faith Berven
Graphic Designers: Alisann Dixon, Linda Ford,
    Lynda Haupert, Lyne Neymeyer, Tom Wegner

Editor in Chief: James A. Autry
Editorial Director: Neil Kuehnl
Group Administrative Editor: Duane Gregg
Executive Art Director: William J. Yates

Shortcut Recipes

Editors: Joy Taylor, Diana Tryon
Copy and Production Editor: David A. Walsh
Graphic Designer: Alisann Dixon

Better Homes and Gardens
TEST KITCHEN ®

Our seal assures you that every recipe in *Shortcut Recipes* is endorsed by the
Better Homes and Gardens Test Kitchen. Each recipe is tested for family appeal,
practicality, and deliciousness.

CONTENTS

STEP-SAVING COOKING
make the most of your time

Step-saving cooking is yours with *Better Homes and Gardens® Shortcut Recipes*. For those occasions when you don't have the time, energy, or desire to spend hours cooking, a quick and easy answer to your dilemma is right here.

Choose from this book's three types of recipes—fast to prepare, easy on the cook, and make-ahead recipes. For a meal in a hurry, prepare a "fast" recipe, such as Spaghetti with Red Clam Sauce, that's ready to eat within 45 minutes. Or, for a quick-to-assemble meal choose an "easy" recipe, such as Oven Pork Stew, that cooks without your attention.

When you have time to cook, turn to Planned-Ahead Main Dishes for foods you prepare now, freeze, then cook and serve later. These include recipes for basic meat mixes you can freeze to use later in accompanying recipes. In this chapter you'll also find recipes for cooked meat and poultry—a great use for leftovers. And each freezer casserole recipe makes more than one casserole, so you do all the work at once for more than one meal. Prepare and freeze them, then heat and serve later.

Chopping, mixing, and basic assembling steps are reduced to a minimum in all recipes. Every shortcut has been taken to make cooking faster and easier for you. You'll also find that classic recipes—including Peppery Meatball Sandwiches, Chicken Tetrazzini, and Lamb Chowder with Dumplings—are simpler to prepare than the traditional methods, yet sacrifice no flavor or appeal.

Preparation timings—accurate estimates of the amount of time needed to prepare a recipe—accompany all recipes. These timings take into account whenever two steps of a recipe can be done at the same time. For example, you often can prepare a sauce while the rice cooks.

On the next few pages you'll learn the basics for shortcutting meal preparation. Read *Shortcut Cooking Tips* and *Kitchen Appliances That Save Time* to make your meal preparation easier. You'll also find *Ingredient Substitutions* that could save you a last-minute trip to the grocery store.

shortcut cooking tips

The recipes in this book, plus these tips, will help you save time and effort in planning, organizing, and preparing meals.

——— Plan meals for several days or a week in advance. By making only one shopping trip to ensure you have all necessary ingredients when preparing the planned meals, you'll eliminate wasted time spent on unnecessary trips.

——— Keep an orderly and efficient kitchen. For faster meal preparation have duplicates of frequently used utensils such as measuring cups and spoons, spatulas, paring knives, mixing spoons, and mixing bowls. Save steps by keeping frequently used equipment close at hand. Store seldom used items in less convenient places.

——— Keep a stock of food to use for last-minute meals. These should include eggs, cheese, milk, meat, pasta, canned or frozen fruits and vegetables, and bread. Also, always keep these shelf-stable foods on hand: flour, sugar, salt, pepper, baking powder, baking soda, coffee, tea, shortening, salad oil, butter, herbs, spices, vanilla, mayonnaise, prepared mustard, Worcestershire sauce, catsup, and instant bouillon granules.

——— Prepare ingredients for several days' recipes all at once. For example, shred cheese and chop vegetables and nuts. Seal the food in plastic bags; then label and store as needed.

——— When available, purchase ingredients in the form needed for a recipe. For example, buy shredded cheese, cut-up chicken, chopped nuts, and cracker crumbs. These foods cost a little more but save you time because you don't have to do the work.

——— Other speed-up-preparation foods are minced dried onion, minced dried garlic, and diced dried bell pepper.

——— Avoid using extra dishes, whenever possible. For example, mix the milk, egg, and oil for muffins in the cup you measure the milk in. Or carefully mix a casserole in its baking dish. Use a saucepan as a mixing bowl besides cooking in it.

——— Foods bake faster in smaller portions. You can cut time by baking meat loaf in muffin pans, custard in small cups, and casseroles in individual baking dishes.

——— Serve one-dish meals such as meat-and-vegetable combinations. They save cooking, serving, and cleanup time. Serve just a salad or a dessert with a simple main dish.

——— Serve cold meals more often. These include salads, sandwiches, and soups. They're as appetizing as hot meals, but take less time to fix.

——— Serve foods in big pieces when possible. For example, serve a wedge of lettuce instead of torn greens for a salad.

——— To separate frozen vegetables quickly, place them in a colander and run hot water over. Add the partially thawed vegetables to casseroles or range-top dishes to finish cooking.

——— Hard-cook eggs several at a time; you'll have them ready to use in salads and casseroles, or for a quick, nutritious snack. Store hard-cooked eggs in the refrigerator for up to one week.

——— Before starting meal preparation, read all recipes thoroughly. You'll also save time by assembling ingredients and utensils before you begin the recipe.

——— "Dovetail" meal preparation—do two jobs at the same time. For instance, while the meat browns, chop the vegetables or make the sauce.

kitchen appliances
that save time

Modern kitchen appliances make cooking easier. If you have a microwave oven, blender, food processor, or pressure saucepan, use it to speed up time-consuming cooking tasks. These appliances, though helpful, are not necessary for preparing the recipes in this book.

blender

Blend, chop, crumb, emulsify, and purée foods in seconds with the aid of a blender. This handy appliance makes many cooking jobs easier—use it often and save time in all your meal preparation.

Dips, spreads, sauces, soups, gravies, and salad dressings are smoother and take less time to prepare when whirled in a blender. Dry bread, crackers, and cookies can be crumbled instantly. Process these foods in small batches, then store in the refrigerator till needed. Easily chop nuts for desserts. And vegetables and fruits can be chopped in water or puréed quickly without making a mess. Hard cheese, such as Parmesan cheese, can be grated in the blender, too.

Blender blades have a fast cutting action rather than a mixing action. The blades create a whirlpool within the container which draws large particles in and out of the blades. The particles become smaller as the blender continues to run. To regulate the size of ingredient pieces, quickly turn the blender off and on when chopping.

food processor

A food processor can do many of the same jobs as the blender, but it is even more versatile. The interchangeable cutting tools provide more control in processing foods to the desired shape and size. A steel blade is used for chopping, puréeing, mixing, and kneading. This blade, plus the slicing disk and the shredding disk, let you efficiently process a wider variety of foods than the blender. Use the processor to shred cheese, chop parsley, chop hard-cooked eggs, slice fruits and vegetables, and chop uncooked meats. Process dry foods before wet ones to save time and to avoid washing the work bowl repeatedly. Also process similar textured foods at the same time.

microwave oven

Use your microwave oven to save time even when you cook a meal conventionally. Quickly melt butter or margarine and chocolate in the microwave oven. Toast nuts and coconut in minutes and speedily defrost frozen foods. Chopped onion or other vegetables quickly cook in butter in the microwave oven. Using the microwave oven for simple cooking tasks also saves on cleanup time, since a container used for micro-cooking often doubles as the mixing container.

Before micro-cooking, read the manufacturer's instructions for operating your microwave oven.

pressure saucepan

These specially designed saucepans cook food under pressure. Steam held under pressure in the saucepan results in a temperature higher than the boiling point of water. Thus, the food cooks in about a third of the time required by conventional boiling or steaming. The short cooking time and the small amount of water used in pressure cooking preserves the nutrients in foods, plus helps tenderize foods such as stew meat.

ingredient substitutions

The following ingredient substitutions should be used *for emergencies only*. For best results, use ingredients specified in the recipe since substitutions can change flavor and texture.

If you don't have:	Substitute:
1 cup cake flour	1 cup minus 2 tablespoons all-purpose flour
1 tablespoon cornstarch (for thickening)	2 tablespoons all-purpose flour
1 teaspoon baking powder	¼ teaspoon baking soda plus ½ cup buttermilk or sour milk (to replace ½ cup liquid called for in recipe)
1 package active dry yeast	1 cake compressed yeast
1 cup granulated sugar	1 cup packed brown sugar *or* 2 cups sifted powdered sugar
1 cup honey	1¼ cups granulated sugar plus ¼ cup liquid
1 cup corn syrup	1 cup granulated sugar plus ¼ cup liquid
1 square (1 ounce) unsweetened chocolate	3 tablespoons unsweetened cocoa powder plus 1 tablespoon butter or margarine
1 cup whipping cream, whipped	2 cups whipped dessert topping
1 cup buttermilk	1 tablespoon lemon juice or vinegar plus enough whole milk to make 1 cup (let stand 5 minutes) *or* 1 cup whole milk plus 1¾ teaspoons cream of tartar *or* 1 cup plain yogurt
1 cup whole milk	½ cup evaporated milk plus ½ cup water *or* 1 cup reconstituted non-fat dry milk (plus 2 teaspoons butter or margarine, if desired)
1 cup light cream	1 cup minus 2 tablespoons milk plus 2 tablespoons butter
1 whole egg	2 egg yolks (for most uses)
2 cups tomato sauce	¾ cup tomato paste plus 1 cup water
1 cup tomato juice	½ cup tomato sauce plus ½ cup water
1 cup catsup or chili sauce	1 cup tomato sauce plus ½ cup sugar and 2 tablespoons vinegar (for use in cooked mixtures)
1 cup broth	1 teaspoon instant bouillon granules dissolved in 1 cup water
1 clove garlic	⅛ teaspoon garlic powder *or* minced dried garlic
1 small onion	1 teaspoon onion powder *or* 1 tablespoon minced dried onion
1 teaspoon dry mustard	1 tablespoon prepared mustard
1 teaspoon finely shredded lemon peel	½ teaspoon lemon extract
1 tablespoon fresh snipped herbs	1 teaspoon dried herbs, crushed

fast-and-easy
MAIN DISHES

No matter how demanding your schedule is, you will find that this chapter has a variety of delicious main dishes guaranteed to make meal preparation easier.

Some recipes are "fast" and can be prepared and served within 45 minutes; others are "easy" and take but minutes to assemble, then cook without your attention. Check the assembling and cooking timings to choose a recipe that fits your timetable.

Recipes for meat, poultry, fish, seafood, egg, and cheese dishes are featured in the four sections of this chapter—*From the Oven, On the Range, Under the Broiler,* and *Salads and Sandwiches.*

Under the Broiler features fast recipes. There you'll also find a meat broiling chart with easy sauce recipes to serve over these broiled meats. *From the Oven* and *On the Range* include both fast and easy recipes. *Salads and Sandwiches* are naturally fast-to-prepare foods; but you'll find our hot and cold salad and sandwich recipes shortcutted so they're extra quick.

Pictured: Try *Broiled Orange Chicken* (see recipe, page 37) which is brushed with an orange marmalade-barbecue sauce. Or, prepare *Fruited Fish Fillets* (see recipe, page 38) which starts with blocks of frozen fish fillets and then topped with a fruit sauce.

from the oven

stroganoff meat loaf

Assembling time: 20 minutes
Cooking time: 1 hour

- **2 beaten eggs**
- **¾ cup milk**
- **1 tablespoon minced dried onion**
- **¼ teaspoon salt**
- **¼ teaspoon pepper**
- **1 1½-ounce envelope stroganoff sauce mix**
- **¼ cup soft bread crumbs**
- **1½ pounds ground beef**
- **1 4-ounce can mushroom stems and pieces, drained and chopped**
- **⅓ cup milk**
- **1 5¾-ounce can steak sauce with mushrooms**
- **2 teaspoons dried parsley flakes**
- **Few dashes paprika**

In bowl combine eggs, ¾ cup milk, dried onion, salt, and pepper. Stir in *half* the dry sauce mix and the bread crumbs. Add meat and mushrooms; mix well. Shape meat mixture into an 8x4-inch loaf in a 13x9x2-inch baking pan; smooth top. Bake, uncovered, in a 350° oven for about 1 hour. Spoon off excess fat. Meanwhile, combine remaining dry sauce mix and ⅓ cup milk. Cook and stir till bubbly. Stir in steak sauce, parsley, and paprika; heat through. Transfer meat loaf to platter; spoon sauce atop. Serves 6.

beef-vegetable puffs

Assembling time: 25 minutes
Cooking time: 35 minutes

- **1 10-ounce package (6) frozen patty shells, thawed**
- **1 cup sliced fresh mushrooms**
- **2 green onions, sliced into ½-inch lengths**
- **½ cup shredded carrot**
- **¼ cup chopped green pepper**
- **2 tablespoons butter**
- **½ pound beef round steak, cut ¼ inch thick and thinly sliced into bite-size pieces**
- **½ cup dairy sour cream**
- **3 tablespoons snipped parsley**
- **2 tablespoons chopped pimiento**
- **¼ teaspoon dried basil, crushed**
- **1 1¾-ounce envelope hollandaise sauce mix**
- **⅛ teaspoon dried basil, crushed**

On lightly floured surface roll each patty shell to a 6-inch circle. In skillet cook mushrooms, onion, carrot, and green pepper in butter till tender; push aside. Add beef; cook and stir over medium-high heat 5 to 6 minutes or till browned. Remove from heat; stir sour cream, *2 tablespoons* parsley, pimiento, ¼ teaspoon basil, ½ teaspoon *salt*, and

dash *pepper* into meat mixture. Place about ⅓ cup mixture on half of each pastry circle. Fold other half of pastry over filling and seal edges with a fork; place on a baking sheet. Bake in 400° oven 25 to 30 minutes or till browned. Meanwhile, prepare sauce according to package directions. Stir in the remaining snipped parsley and ⅛ teaspoon basil; spoon over puffs. Serves 3.

luau meat loaf

Assembling time: 20 minutes
Cooking time: 1¼ hours

- **1 8¼-ounce can pineapple slices, drained**
- **1 beaten egg**
- **⅓ cup catsup**
- **2 tablespoons soy sauce**
- **½ cup finely crushed saltine crackers (14 crackers)**
- **½ cup chopped onion**
- **⅓ cup chopped green pepper**
- **½ teaspoon ground ginger**
- **1½ pounds ground beef**

Cut 2 pineapple slices in half; chop remaining pineapple. Combine egg, catsup, soy sauce, crushed crackers, onion, green pepper, and ginger. Add meat and chopped pineapple; mix well. Pat meat mixture into an 8x4x2-inch loaf pan. Arrange halved pineapple slices atop meat, pressing in lightly. Bake in a 350° oven for 1¼ hours. Serves 6.

beef and bean tortillas

Assembling time: 20 minutes
Cooking time: 20 minutes

10 *or* **12 flour tortillas**
 1 pound ground beef *or*
    ground pork
 1 medium onion, chopped
 1 16-ounce can refried
    beans
 1 7½-ounce can tomatoes,
    cut up
 3 tablespoons chopped
    canned green chili
    peppers
 ¼ teaspoon garlic powder
 ¼ teaspoon salt
 1 cup shredded cheddar
    cheese (4 ounces)
    Bottled taco sauce

Wrap tortillas in foil. Place in a
325° oven for 15 minutes or till
ready to serve.

Meanwhile, in skillet cook
ground beef or ground pork
and onion till meat is browned
and onion is tender. Drain off
fat. Stir in beans, *undrained*
tomatoes, chili peppers, garlic
powder, and salt; heat
through.

To serve, spoon about ⅓
cup bean mixture atop each
warm tortilla. Roll up tortillas.
Place in 13x9x2-inch baking
pan. Bake, covered, in a 325°
oven for 15 minutes. Top with
the cheese and taco sauce.
Bake, uncovered, 5 minutes
more or till cheese is melted.
Makes 5 or 6 servings.

tamale bake

Assembling time: 15 minutes
Cooking time: 45 minutes

 1 15-ounce can tamales
 2 tablespoons all-purpose
    flour
 1 teaspoon chili powder
 ¼ teaspoon garlic salt
 3 beaten eggs
 1 17-ounce can cream-style
    corn
 ½ cup pitted ripe olives,
    halved
 ½ cup shredded sharp
    cheddar cheese
    (2 ounces)

Drain and unwrap tamales, reserving sauce. Slice tamales
crosswise; set aside. In mixing
bowl combine reserved tamale
sauce, flour, chili powder,
garlic salt, and ¼ teaspoon
salt. Add eggs, corn, olives,
and sliced tamales. Turn into a
10x6x2-inch baking dish. Bake,
uncovered, in a 350° oven for
40 minutes or till set. Sprinkle
with cheese. Bake 3 minutes
more or till cheese is melted.
Cut into squares to serve.
Makes 4 servings.

pizza pie

Assembling time: 20 minutes
Cooking time: 20 minutes

 2 3½-ounce packages
    sliced pepperoni *or* **7**
    ounces sliced salami
 1 package (8) refrigerated
    crescent rolls
 1½ cups shredded
    mozzarella cheese
    (6 ounces)
 ½ cup pizza sauce
 1 4-ounce can sliced
    mushrooms, drained
 ½ cup pitted ripe olives,
    halved

Halve the pepperoni or salami
slices. Unroll crescent rolls,
separating along perforations.
Press 5 crescent dough pieces
onto the bottom and up the
sides of a 9-inch pie plate.
Sprinkle ½ cup of the cheese
atop. Spoon ¼ *cup* pizza
sauce over all. Place pepperoni or salami, mushrooms, and
olives atop. Spoon on remaining pizza sauce. Sprinkle remaining cheese atop. Cover
top of pie with remaining crescent dough; crimp edges.
Bake in a 400° oven for 18 to
20 minutes or till crust is
brown. Cut into wedges to
serve. Makes 6 servings.

11

from the oven

ham-sauerkraut casserole

Assembling time:10 minutes
Cooking time: 25 minutes

**2 cups chopped fully
    cooked ham**
**1 16-ounce can sauerkraut,
    rinsed, drained, and
    snipped**
**1 10¾-ounce can
    condensed cream of
    potato soup**
**1 cup shredded Swiss
    cheese**
½ cup milk
**1 tablespoon prepared
    mustard**
½ teaspoon caraway seed
¾ cup rye bread crumbs
**1 tablespoon butter *or*
    margarine, melted**

Combine ham, sauerkraut,
soup, cheese, milk, mustard,
and caraway. Turn mixture
into five 10-ounce casseroles.
Stir together crumbs and butter; sprinkle atop casseroles.
Bake, uncovered, in a 375°
oven 25 minutes. Serves 5.
Microwave directions
Combine ham, sauerkraut,
soup, cheese, milk, mustard,
and caraway in a 1½-quart
nonmetallic casserole. Cook in
a countertop microwave oven
on high power for 5 minutes.
Stir mixture. Stir together
bread crumbs and melted butter; sprinkle atop casserole.
Micro-cook about 4 minutes
more or till heated through.

oven pork stew

Assembling time: 25 minutes
Cooking time: 1¾ hours

**1 10-ounce package frozen
    succotash**
**1½ pounds boneless lean
    pork, cut into 1-inch
    cubes**
**2 large carrots, thinly
    sliced**
**2 large potatoes, peeled
    and cut into 1-inch
    chunks**
**1 small green pepper,
    chopped**
1 medium onion, chopped
**1 8-ounce can tomato
    sauce**
**1 7½-ounce can tomatoes,
    cut up**
**2 tablespoons quick-
    cooking tapioca**
**1 teaspoon instant beef
    bouillon granules**
**½ teaspoon dried oregano,
    crushed**
**½ teaspoon dried basil,
    crushed**

Run hot water over frozen succotash in colander to partially
thaw; break vegetables apart.
In 3-quart casserole combine
succotash, the pork, carrots,
potatoes, green pepper, onion,
tomato sauce, *undrained* tomatoes, tapioca, bouillon granules, oregano, basil, ½ teaspoon *salt*, and ⅛ teaspoon
pepper. Stir. Bake, covered, in
a 325° oven about 1¾ hours.
Skim off excess fat; stir before serving. Serves 6 to 8.

ham and baked beans with pineapple

Assembling time: 10 minutes
Cooking time: 30 minutes

**2 18-ounce cans baked
    beans in brown sugar
    sauce**
**1 8-ounce can crushed
    pineapple, drained**
⅓ cup catsup
**2 teaspoons minced dried
    onion**
**2 teaspoons
    Worcestershire sauce**
**Few dashes bottled hot
    pepper sauce**
**2 cups chopped fully
    cooked ham**
**1 8¼-ounce can pineapple
    slices, drained**

In bowl combine beans in
brown-sugar sauce, crushed
pineapple, catsup, onion,
Worcestershire sauce, and hot
pepper sauce; stir in ham.
Turn mixture into a 2-quart
casserole. Bake, uncovered, in
375° oven for 20 minutes. Stir
mixture. Top with pineapple
slices. Bake, uncovered, 10
minutes more or till heated
through. Makes 6 servings.

Oven Pork Stew and *Refrig-a-
Rise Rye Bread* (see recipe,
page 80) make an easy, yet
hearty meal.

from the oven

lime chicken

Assembling time: 15 minutes
Cooking time: 80 minutes

2½ cups chicken broth
½ cup chopped onion
½ teaspoon finely
      shredded lime peel
3 tablespoons lime juice
2 tablespoons honey
1 teaspoon salt
½ teaspoon dried mint
      flakes, crushed
⅛ teaspoon pepper
1 cup long grain rice
1 2½- to 3-pound broiler-
      fryer chicken, cut up
2 tablespoons toasted,
      sliced almonds
      Thin lime slices

In saucepan combine chicken broth, onion, lime peel, lime juice, honey, salt, mint, and pepper; bring to boiling. Place rice in a 12x7½x2-inch baking dish; pour about *half* of the hot broth mixture over rice. Arrange chicken pieces atop rice. Pour remaining broth mixture over all. Bake, covered, in a 350° oven for 1¼ hours. Uncover. Top chicken with almonds and lime slices; bake 5 minutes more. Makes 6 servings.

oniony oven-fried chicken

Assembling time: 10 minutes
Cooking time: 50 minutes

⅓ cup fine dry bread
      crumbs
2 tablespoons *regular*
      onion soup mix
1 tablespoon dried parsley
      flakes
2 medium chicken breasts,
      halved lengthwise
2 tablespoons butter *or*
      margarine, melted

In bowl combine bread crumbs, dry onion soup mix, and parsley flakes. Brush chicken breasts with melted butter or margarine, then roll in bread crumb mixture. Place chicken, skin side up without touching, in an ungreased shallow baking pan. Drizzle any remaining butter and sprinkle any remaining bread crumb mixture onto chicken. Bake in a 375° oven about 50 minutes or till tender. Do not turn. Makes 4 servings.

orange-spiced chicken

Total time: 40 minutes

1 32-ounce package frozen
      fried chicken pieces
1 cup cranberry-orange
      relish
¼ cup chili sauce
¼ cup orange juice

Arrange chicken pieces in a single layer in an ungreased 13x9x2-inch baking pan. Bake, uncovered, in a 375° oven for 25 minutes. Meanwhile, combine remaining ingredients; spoon over chicken. Bake, uncovered, 10 minutes more or till heated through. Makes 4 or 5 servings.

SHORTCUT TIP: FROZEN CHOPPED ONION

To save time during recipe preparation, use frozen chopped onion rather than chopping fresh onion every time it is needed.

Commercially frozen chopped onion is available in a 12-ounce package. Or, you can chop a large quantity of fresh onions and freeze portions in small moisture-vapor-proof bags.

One medium onion, chopped, yields ½ cup.

chicken and dressing strata

Assembling time: 10 minutes
Cooking time: 35 minutes

2 slightly beaten eggs
1 cup milk
1 tablespoon dried parsley flakes
2 teaspoons minced dried onion
¼ teaspoon salt
¼ teaspoon poultry seasoning
¼ teaspoon dried thyme, crushed
⅛ teaspoon pepper
2 5-ounce cans boned chicken, drained and chopped, *or* 1¼ cups finely chopped cooked chicken
2 cups herb-seasoned stuffing croutons
1 4-ounce package (1 cup) shredded sharp cheddar cheese

Combine eggs, milk, parsley flakes, onion, salt, poultry seasoning, thyme, and pepper. Stir in chicken, croutons, and *½ cup* of the cheese. Turn mixture into an 8x1½-inch round baking pan. Bake, uncovered, in a 350° oven for 25 minutes. Sprinkle the remaining ½ cup cheese around side edge of dish; bake 3 to 4 minutes more or till cheese is melted. Let stand 5 minutes before serving. Makes 4 servings.

inside-out stuffed chicken

Assembling time: 15 minutes
Cooking time: 1 hour

1 8-ounce package corn bread stuffing mix
¼ cup butter *or* margarine, melted
1 10¾-ounce can condensed cream of chicken soup
⅓ cup milk
1 2½- to 3-pound broiler-fryer chicken, cut up

In a large bowl combine corn bread stuffing mix and melted butter or margarine; toss well. In medium bowl stir together soup and milk. Dip chicken into soup mixture then into stuffing mixture, pressing with hands to coat chicken pieces.

Place coated chicken pieces in a 15½x10½x2-inch baking pan. Bake in a 375° oven about 1 hour or till done. Makes 6 servings.

cranberry turkey roast

Total time: 2 hours

1 2-pound frozen boneless turkey roast (without gravy)
1 8-ounce can whole cranberry sauce
2 tablespoons burgundy
1 tablespoon brown sugar
1½ teaspoons prepared mustard

Roast frozen turkey roast according to package directions till meat thermometer inserted in center reaches 170°. Meanwhile, in a saucepan combine whole cranberry sauce, burgundy, brown sugar, and mustard. Simmer, uncovered, for 5 minutes. Remove from heat.

Spoon half of the cranberry-wine sauce over turkey roast during the last 20 minutes of roasting. Continue roasting till turkey is done. Let roast stand 10 minutes before carving. Pass remaining sauce. Makes 4 to 6 servings.

Crockery cooker directions
Thaw frozen turkey roast. Line the inside of electric slow crockery cooker with foil; place turkey in cooker. Cover and cook on low-heat setting for 8 hours. Just before serving, prepare the sauce as above.

To serve, remove cooked turkey to serving platter; let stand 10 minutes before carving. Spoon some of the sauce over turkey; pass remainder.

15

from the oven

baked fish and broccoli

Total time: 45 minutes

1 16-ounce package frozen fish fillets
1 10-ounce package frozen broccoli spears
1 medium onion, chopped
2 tablespoons butter
2 tablespoons all-purpose flour
1 teaspoon prepared mustard
1 cup milk
1 teaspoon instant chicken bouillon granules
1 2-ounce can sliced mushrooms, drained
1 tablespoon lemon juice

Let fish stand at room temperature 15 minutes. Meanwhile, run hot water over frozen broccoli in collander to thaw partially. Wrap broccoli in foil. Place in 450° oven for 10 minutes. Cut fish into 4 pieces. Arrange fish in a greased shallow baking pan; season. Continue baking broccoli and bake the fish in 450° oven for 25 to 30 minutes or till fish flakes.

Meanwhile, for sauce, cook onion in butter till tender. Stir in flour, mustard, ¼ teaspoon *salt*, and dash *pepper*. Add milk and the bouillon granules. Cook and stir till bubbly. Cook and stir 1 to 2 minutes more. Stir in mushrooms and lemon juice. Spoon sauce over fish and broccoli. Sprinkle with *paprika*. Serves 4.

dilled salmon casserole

Assembling time: 15 minutes
Cooking time: 25 minutes

1 15½-ounce can salmon
1 5⅓-ounce can evaporated milk
½ cup sliced water chestnuts
½ cup quick-cooking rice
½ cup finely crushed saltine crackers
¼ cup water
2 teaspoons minced dried onion
2 teaspoons dried parsley flakes
2 teaspoons lemon juice
½ teaspoon dried dillweed Dash pepper
¼ cup shredded Swiss cheese

Drain salmon, reserving liquid. Remove skin and bones. Flake salmon. In bowl stir together flaked salmon, reserved liquid, evaporated milk, water chestnuts, uncooked rice, crushed crackers, water, dried onion, dried parsley, lemon juice, dillweed, and pepper. Turn into a 1-quart casserole. Bake, covered, in a 350° oven about 20 minutes or till rice is tender. Sprinkle with cheese. Bake, uncovered, for 5 minutes more or till cheese is melted. Makes 4 servings.

seafood louisiana

Assembling time: 20 minutes
Cooking time: 25 minutes

1 9-ounce package frozen artichoke hearts
1 tablespoon butter *or* margarine
1 tablespoon all-purpose flour
1 10½-ounce can condensed oyster stew
1 teaspoon minced dried onion
1 cup cooked rice
1 4½-ounce can shrimp, drained
¾ cup soft bread crumbs (1 slice bread)
1 tablespoon butter *or* margarine, melted

Cook artichoke hearts according to package directions *except* omit the salt; drain. In a large saucepan melt 1 tablespoon butter or margarine; blend in flour. Stir in oyster stew and onion. Cook and stir till mixture thickens and bubbles. Remove from heat; stir in rice, shrimp, and artichoke hearts. Turn into two 2½-cup casseroles. Combine bread crumbs and remaining butter or margarine; sprinkle around edge of casseroles. Bake, uncovered, in 350° oven about 25 minutes. Makes 2 servings.

16

tuna divan

Assembling time: 20 minutes
Cooking time: 15 minutes

**1 10-ounce package frozen
 cut asparagus *or*
 chopped broccoli**
1 medium onion, chopped
**2 tablespoons butter *or*
 margarine**
**2 tablespoons all-purpose
 flour**
**¼ teaspoon dried thyme,
 crushed**
1 cup milk
**½ cup grated Parmesan
 cheese**
**3 tablespoons dry white
 wine**
**2 6½-ounce cans tuna,
 drained**
**6 rich round crackers,
 crushed (¼ cup)**

Cook asparagus or broccoli
according to package directions; drain. Meanwhile, in
saucepan cook onion in butter
or margarine till tender. Blend
in flour, thyme, ¼ teaspoon
salt, and ⅛ teaspoon *pepper*.
Add milk. Cook and stir till
thickened and bubbly. Stir in
¼ cup Parmesan cheese. Remove saucepan from heat. Stir
in wine. Arrange asparagus or
broccoli in four au gratin
dishes. Add tuna. Top with
sauce. Combine remaining
Parmesan cheese and crushed
crackers; sprinkle over sauce.
Bake in a 350° oven about 15
minutes or till heated through.
Makes 4 servings.

cheddar cheese puff

Assembling time: 5 minutes
Cooking time: 50 minutes

5 eggs
⅓ cup milk
**1 teaspoon minced dried
 onion**
**⅛ teaspoon crushed red
 pepper**
**1 8-ounce package cream
 cheese, cubed**
**6 ounces cheddar cheese,
 cubed (1½ cups)**

In blender container or food
processor bowl combine eggs,
milk, dried onion, and red pepper. Cover and blend till
smooth. With blender or food
processor running, add cheese
cubes through opening in lid
and process till nearly smooth.
Pour cheese mixture into an
ungreased 1-quart soufflé dish
or other straight-sided casserole. Bake in a 375° oven
about 50 minutes or till puffy
and set. (Puff will remain
creamy in center.) Serve immediately. Makes 4 servings.

vegetable-cheese strata

Assembling time: 20 minutes
Cooking time: 1¼ hours

3 cups Italian bread cubes
8 slices Swiss cheese
**1 10-ounce package frozen
 peas**
**1 2-ounce can chopped
 mushrooms, drained**
4 eggs
**1 10¾-ounce can
 condensed cream of
 onion soup**
1 cup milk
**⅓ cup fine dry bread
 crumbs**
**1 tablespoon butter *or*
 margarine, melted**

Arrange bread cubes in a
9x9x2-inch baking pan. Top
with *half* of the cheese. Break
up frozen peas; place on
cheese layer along with mushrooms. Place remaining
cheese atop. Beat eggs; stir in
soup, milk, and ⅛ teaspoon
pepper. Pour over casserole.
Combine bread crumbs and
butter; sprinkle over all.
 Bake, uncovered, in a 325°
oven 65 minutes or till set. Let
stand 10 minutes. Serves 6.
Make ahead directions
Combine ingredients as above
except do not sprinkle buttered bread crumbs atop. Chill
up to 24 hours. To bake,
sprinkle buttered bread
crumbs atop. Bake as above,
adding 10 minutes to total
baking time.

17

from the oven

cheese-broccoli casserole

Assembling time: 20 minutes
Cooking time: 30 minutes

- **1 10-ounce package frozen broccoli spears *or* ½ pound fresh broccoli, cut into spears**
- **1 cup quick-cooking rice**
- **1 tablespoon minced dried onion**
- **2 beaten eggs**
- **½ cup ricotta cheese**
- **½ cup shredded mozzarella cheese (2 ounces)**
- **1 2-ounce can sliced pimiento, chopped**
- **½ cup milk**
- **1 cup shredded cheddar cheese (4 ounces)**

Cook frozen broccoli according to package directions; drain. (Or, cook fresh broccoli spears, covered, in 1 inch of boiling salted water for 10 to 15 minutes or till crisp-tender; drain well.) Meanwhile, prepare rice with the dried onion according to rice package directions.

Combine cooked rice, eggs, ricotta cheese, mozzarella cheese, pimiento, ½ teaspoon *salt*, and dash *pepper*. Stir in milk. Turn mixture into a 10-inch pie plate or quiche dish. Arrange broccoli atop. Sprinkle cheddar cheese in center. Bake in a 350° oven 20 minutes or till almost set. Let stand 10 minutes. Serves 4.

Prepare *Cheese-Broccoli Casserole* for a meatless main dish made in only 50 minutes.

filled puffy pancake

Total time: 35 minutes

- **3 tablespoons butter *or* margarine**
- **4 eggs**
- **⅔ cup all-purpose flour**
- **⅔ cup milk**
- **¼ teaspoon dried marjoram, crushed**
- **1 cup milk**
- **2 tablespoons all-purpose flour**
- **1 teaspoon Worcestershire sauce**
- **½ cup shredded cheddar cheese (2 ounces)**
- **1 cup cubed fully cooked ham**
- **1 8-ounce can cut green beans, drained**

Melt the butter in a 10-inch ovenproof skillet. In bowl combine eggs, ⅔ cup flour, ⅔ cup milk, marjoram, ¼ teaspoon *salt*, and dash *pepper*; beat with rotary beater till smooth. Pour the batter into the hot skillet. Bake in a 400° oven for 20 minutes or till puffy.

Meanwhile, prepare sauce. In screw-top jar combine 1 cup milk, 2 tablespoons all-purpose flour, Worcestershire sauce, and dash *pepper*. Cook and stir mixture in saucepan over medium heat till thickened and bubbly. Stir in cheese. Add ham and beans; heat through.

To serve, spoon sauce into center of pancake. Serves 6.

saucy blue cheese puff

Assembling time: 15 minutes
Cooking time: 30 minutes

- **1 10-ounce package frozen peas and carrots**
- **1 cup water**
- **1 teaspoon instant chicken bouillon granules**
- **½ cup light cream *or* milk**
- **3 tablespoons cornstarch**
- **5 eggs**
- **⅓ cup light cream *or* milk**
- **⅛ teaspoon pepper**
- **1 cup crumbled blue cheese (4 ounces)**
- **1 8-ounce package cream cheese, cubed**

Cook peas and carrots in the water and bouillon granules till tender; do not drain. Combine ½ cup light cream or milk and cornstarch; add to vegetables. Add ¼ teaspoon *salt;* cook and stir till thickened and bubbly. Turn into an 8x1½-inch round baking dish.

In blender container or food processor bowl combine eggs, ⅓ cup light cream or milk, and pepper. Cover and blend till smooth. With blender or processor running, add cheeses through opening in lid and process till smooth. Pour cheese mixture carefully over the vegetable mixture in baking dish. Bake in a 375° oven about 30 minutes or till puffy and set. To serve, cut into wedges; spoon vegetable sauce over. Serves 5.

on the range

mexican beef

Assembling time: 15 minutes
Cooking time: 35 minutes

**1 pound beef round steak,
  cut into thin bite-size
  strips**
**1 15-ounce can pinto
  beans, drained**
**1 11-ounce can condensed
  cheddar cheese soup**
**1 10-ounce package frozen
  whole kernel corn**
**1 8-ounce can tomato
  sauce**
**1 2¼-ounce can sliced
  pitted ripe olives,
  drained (½ cup)**
**2 tablespoons chopped
  canned green chili
  peppers**
**½ of a 1¼-ounce envelope
  taco seasoning mix**
Corn chips
Dairy sour cream

In Dutch oven combine beef,
pinto beans, condensed soup,
frozen corn, tomato sauce,
olives, chili peppers, and taco
seasoning mix. Bring to boiling
over medium-high heat, stirring often. Reduce heat; cover
and simmer 30 minutes, stirring occasionally. Remove
cover; continue simmering 5
minutes more, stirring often.
Turn into serving bowls; pass
corn chips and sour cream.
Makes 6 servings.

cubed steaks with peppers

Assembling time: 10 minutes
Cooking time: 25 minutes

4 beef cubed steaks
2 tablespoons cooking oil
**1 7½-ounce can tomatoes,
  cut up**
**2 medium green peppers,
  cut into strips**
**1 small onion, sliced and
  separated into rings**
**½ teaspoon dried basil,
  crushed**
**¼ teaspoon dried oregano,
  crushed**
¼ cup cold water
**1 tablespoon all-purpose
  flour**

Season meat with salt and
pepper. In large skillet brown
meat on both sides in hot oil;
drain off fat. Add *undrained*
tomatoes, the green peppers,
onion, basil, oregano, and ¼
teaspoon *salt*. Cover and simmer about 20 minutes. Re-
move meat to serving platter.
Blend together cold water and
flour; stir into mixture in skillet.
Cook and stir till thickened and
bubbly. Cook 1 to 2 minutes
more. Serve mixture over
meat. Serves 4.

steak with onion-wine sauce

Total time: 20 minutes

**6 beef tenderloin steaks,
  cut 1 inch thick
  (1¾ pounds total)**
**1 tablespoon butter *or*
  margarine**
1 tablespoon olive oil
¼ cup sliced green onion
½ cup dry red wine
**2 tablespoons snipped
  parsley**
½ teaspoon salt
Dash pepper
**2 tablespoons butter *or*
  margarine**

In 10-inch skillet cook steaks
in the 1 tablespoon butter and
the olive oil over medium-high
heat to desired doneness,
turning once. (Allow 9 to 10
minutes total cooking time for
rare; 11 to 12 minutes for medium.) Season steaks with a
little salt and pepper. Transfer
to serving platter; keep warm.
  In same skillet cook green
onion in drippings till tender
but not brown. Add wine, parsley, ½ teaspoon salt, and
dash pepper to skillet; stir to
loosen crusty bits from bottom
of pan. Heat and stir till sauce
is bubbly. Stir in 2 tablespoons
butter just till melted. Serve
immediately over hot steaks.
Makes 6 servings.

veal veronica

Total time: 20 minutes

**6 veal chops, cut ¾ inch
     thick (1¾ pounds total)**
1 tablespoon cooking oil
⅓ cup dry white wine
¼ cup water
2 teaspoons cornstarch
**¾ teaspoon instant chicken
     bouillon granules**
**1 tablespoon snipped
     parsley**
**1 tablespoon chopped
     green onion**
**½ cup halved seedless
     green grapes**
1 teaspoon lemon juice

In 12-inch skillet cook veal
chops over medium-high heat
in hot oil 6 to 7 minutes per
side. Remove chops to serving
platter; keep warm. Combine
wine, water, cornstarch, and
bouillon granules; stir into drippings in skillet. Add parsley
and onion. Cook and stir till
thickened and bubbly. Stir in
grapes and lemon juice; cook
1 minute more or till grapes
are heated through. Spoon
sauce over chops. Makes 6
servings.

pork chops and rice

Assembling time: 15 minutes
Cooking time: 25 minutes

**4 pork loin chops, cut ¾
     inch thick (about 1¾
     pounds total)**
1 tablespoon cooking oil
1 cup long grain rice
1 small onion, chopped
**1 small green pepper, cut
     into strips**
1½ cups water
**1 7½-ounce can tomatoes,
     cut up**
**1 tablespoon instant
     chicken bouillon
     granules**
½ teaspoon ground sage
**¼ teaspoon dried
     rosemary, crushed**
⅛ teaspoon ground pepper
**1 8-ounce can diced
     carrots, drained**

Trim fat from chops. In a 12-
inch skillet slowly brown chops
on both sides in hot oil (about
10 minutes total). Remove
chops from skillet; sprinkle
chops with salt. In same skillet
combine uncooked rice, onion,
and green pepper; add water,
undrained tomatoes, bouillon
granules, sage, rosemary, and
pepper. Place chops atop rice
mixture. Cover and simmer
about 20 minutes or till rice is
tender. Spoon carrots around
chops. Cover and simmer 5
minutes more or till carrots are
heated through. Makes 4
servings.

mushroom-topped muffins

Assembling time: 10 minutes
Cooking time: 15 minutes

**8 slices Canadian-style
     bacon**
**2 tablespoons butter *or*
     margarine**
**3 cups whole fresh
     mushrooms, sliced**
¼ cup chopped onion
¾ cup dairy sour cream
**1 tablespoon all-purpose
     flour**
¼ cup milk
½ teaspoon paprika
½ teaspoon lemon juice
**4 English muffins, split,
     toasted, and buttered**

In skillet brown Canadian-style
bacon in butter or margarine.
Remove from skillet and keep
warm. Cook mushrooms and
onion in skillet drippings till
tender but not brown. Drain
off excess liquid. Meanwhile,
combine sour cream and flour.
Stir milk, paprika and lemon
juice into sour cream; add to
mushroom mixture in skillet.
Heat through, stirring constantly (*do not boil*). Season
to taste. Place one slice bacon
atop each muffin half; spoon
mushroom mixture atop. Serve
immediately. Makes 4
servings.

21

on the range

ham hodgepodge

Assembling time: 15 minutes
Cooking time: 1¼ hours

- **1 medium head cabbage, coarsely chopped**
- **6 large carrots, cut into 1-inch pieces**
- **2 large potatoes, peeled and chopped**
- **2 cups diced fully cooked ham**
- **1 medium onion, chopped**
- **3 cups water**
- **½ teaspoon salt**
- **½ teaspoon seasoned salt**
- **⅛ teaspoon pepper**
- **1 15-ounce can garbanzo beans**

In large saucepan combine all ingredients *except* garbanzo beans. Cover; simmer 1 hour. Add *undrained* garbanzo beans. Cook, covered, 10 to 15 minutes more. (Add more water, if necessary.) Serves 6.

SHORTCUT TIP: FROZEN MEAT

To roast frozen meat, add ⅓ to ½ more time as needed to roast fresh meat. To broil frozen steaks, chops, or patties, place the meat 4 to 5 inches from heat to allow even cooking without burning. Broil until desired doneness.

ham and cheese stacks

Assembling time: 10 minutes
Cooking time: 10 minutes

- **⅔ cup fine dry bread crumbs**
- **1 tablespoon snipped parsley**
- **⅛ teaspoon pepper**
- **1 16-ounce can ham patties**
- **½ cup all-purpose flour**
- **1 beaten egg**
- **¼ cup butter *or* margarine**
- **8 thin slices tomato**
- **4 slices Swiss cheese, halved (4 ounces)**

Combine bread crumbs, parsley, and pepper. Dip ham patties in the flour, then in the beaten egg. Coat patties with the crumb mixture.

In 12-inch skillet cook patties in butter or margarine over medium-high heat about 4 minutes on each side or till golden brown. Top each ham patty with a tomato slice, then with a half slice of cheese. Cover and heat 2 minutes or till cheese is melted. Makes 8 servings.

sausage-corn spaghetti sauce

Assembling time: 15 minutes
Cooking time: 25 minutes

- **1 pound bulk pork sausage**
- **1 cup chopped celery**
- **1 medium onion, chopped**
- **1 1⅜-ounce envelope spaghetti sauce mix**
- **1 8¾-ounce can cream-style corn**
- **1 6-ounce can tomato paste**
- **1 3¼-ounce can sliced ripe olives (¾ cup)**
- **Hot cooked fettucini, linguini, *or* spaghetti**

In large saucepan cook sausage, celery, and onion till meat is browned and vegetables are tender. Drain off fat. Stir in spaghetti sauce mix. Add the corn, tomato paste, olives, and 1¾ cups water. Simmer, uncovered, 20 minutes, stirring occasionally. Serve over hot cooked fettucini. Makes 4 servings.

Microwave directions
In a 2-quart nonmetal casserole combine sausage, celery, and onion. Cook, covered, in a countertop microwave oven on high power for 9 minutes or till meat and vegetables are tender, stirring twice. Drain off fat. Stir in spaghetti sauce mix. Add the corn, tomato paste, olives, and 1½ cups water. Micro-cook, covered, 5 minutes or till heated through, stirring twice. Serve as above.

sausage, cheese, and pasta skillet

Assembling time: 20 minutes
Cooking time: 20 minutes

- **4 ounces wide noodles**
- **1 pound bulk pork sausage**
- **1 medium onion, chopped**
- **1 15½-ounce can pizza sauce**
- **1½ cups cream-style cottage cheese**
- **1 4-ounce can sliced mushrooms, drained**
- **¼ cup grated Parmesan cheese**
- **1 6-ounce package sliced mozzarella cheese, cut into triangles**

Cook noodles according to package directions; drain. Meanwhile, in 12-inch skillet cook pork sausage and onion till meat is browned and onion is tender. Drain off fat. Stir in pizza sauce, cottage cheese, mushrooms, and Parmesan cheese. Cover and simmer 15 minutes. Stir in cooked noodles. Arrange mozzarella cheese atop. Cook, covered, 5 minutes more or till cheese is melted. Serve immediately. Makes 6 servings.

hot smoky potato salad

Assembling time: 10 minutes
Cooking time: 25 minutes

- **2 slices bacon**
- **12 ounces fully cooked smoked sausage, sliced**
- **1 medium onion, chopped**
- **1 10¾-ounce can condensed cream of celery soup**
- **¼ cup water**
- **2 tablespoons sweet pickle relish**
- **2 tablespoons vinegar**
- **¼ teaspoon salt**
- **1 16-ounce package frozen french-fried potatoes, halved crosswise**

In 10-inch skillet cook bacon till crisp; set bacon aside, reserving drippings in skillet. Cook sausage and onion in drippings about 5 minutes or till meat is browned and onion is tender. Stir in soup, water, pickle relish, vinegar, and salt; bring to boiling. Add potatoes; cook, covered, for 10 minutes, stirring once or twice. To serve crumble the bacon over potato salad. Serves 4.

saucy lamb meatballs

Assembling time: 15 minutes
Cooking time: 30 minutes

- **1 beaten egg**
- **¼ cup orange juice**
- **¾ cup soft bread crumbs**
- **¾ teaspoon salt**
- **⅛ teaspoon ground cinnamon**
- **1 pound ground lamb**
- **2 tablespoons cooking oil**
- **1 10¾-ounce can condensed cream of mushroom soup**
- **1 2-ounce can sliced mushrooms, drained**
- **½ cup orange juice**
- **¼ cup water**
- **Dash pepper**
- **½ cup dairy sour cream**
- **2 teaspoons all-purpose flour**
- **Hot cooked noodles**

Combine egg, ¼ cup orange juice, bread crumbs, salt, cinnamon, and ⅛ teaspoon *pepper*. Add lamb; mix well. Shape into 1½-inch meatballs. In large skillet brown meatballs in hot oil. Drain off fat. Combine soup, mushrooms, ½ cup orange juice, water, and dash pepper; pour over meatballs. Bring to boiling. Cover and simmer for 15 to 20 minutes. Stir together sour cream and flour; add to meatball mixture. Cook and stir till thickened and bubbly. Cook 2 minutes more. Serve with hot cooked noodles. Makes 4 or 5 servings.

23

on the range

dill-sauced chicken livers with artichokes

Assembling time: 10 minutes
Cooking time: 15 minutes

1 9-ounce package frozen artichoke hearts
¼ cup chopped onion
2 tablespoons butter *or* margarine
16 ounces chicken livers, halved
1 1⅛-ounce envelope hollandaise sauce mix
½ teaspoon dried dillweed
¼ teaspoon salt
⅔ cup water
Hot cooked rice

Cook frozen artichoke hearts according to package directions; set aside. Meanwhile, in 10-inch skillet cook onion in butter or margarine till tender but not brown. Add chicken livers; cook quickly about 4 minutes or just till chicken livers are browned. Remove skillet from heat. Push chicken livers to one side.

Blend dry sauce mix with pan drippings in skillet; add dillweed and salt. Stir in water. Cook and stir over medium heat till thickened and bubbly. Add artichokes; reduce heat and simmer, covered, till heated through. Serve over hot cooked rice. Makes 4 servings.

liver-vegetable dutch puff

Assembling time: 20 minutes
Cooking time: 25 minutes

7 tablespoons butter
3 beaten eggs
½ cup all-purpose flour
½ cup milk
½ cup chicken broth
½ teaspoon dried tarragon, crushed
½ of a 20-ounce package (2 cups) frozen mixed broccoli, cauliflower, and carrots
2 medium tomatoes, peeled, cored, and cut up
2 teaspoons cornstarch
1 medium onion, chopped
1 clove garlic, minced
12 ounces chicken livers

In a 10-inch oven-going skillet melt *4 tablespoons* of the butter, coating bottom. In bowl combine eggs, flour, milk, and ¼ teaspoon *salt;* beat smooth. Stir in butter from skillet. Beat smooth; pour into skillet. Bake in 450° oven for 15 minutes. Reduce oven to 350°; bake 5 to 10 minutes more.

Meanwhile, bring chicken broth, tarragon, and ¼ teaspoon *salt* to boiling; add the frozen vegetables. Simmer, covered, 9 to 10 minutes or till crisp-tender. Stir in tomatoes. Combine cornstarch and 1 tablespoon cold *water;* stir into vegetable mixture. Cook and stir till thickened and bubbly.

Cook and stir 1 to 2 minutes more. Keep warm.

In another skillet cook onion and garlic in the remaining butter till tender. Halve chicken livers; add to skillet. Cook about 5 minutes or till slightly pink in center. Season. Fold into vegetable mixture; spoon into puff. Cut into wedges. Serves 6.

sweet and sour chicken

Assembling time: 15 minutes
Cooking time: 30 minutes

¼ cup all-purpose flour
½ teaspoon salt
Dash pepper
1 2½- to 3-pound broiler-fryer chicken, cut up
2 tablespoons cooking oil
1 8¼-ounce can crushed pineapple
½ cup bottled barbecue sauce
½ teaspoon ground ginger
Hot cooked rice

Combine flour, salt, and pepper; coat chicken. In 10-inch skillet brown chicken, half at a time, in hot oil. Return all chicken to skillet. Combine *undrained* pineapple, barbecue sauce, and ginger; add to chicken. Cover and simmer about 30 minutes or till chicken is tender. Serve with hot cooked rice. Serves 6.

Use an oven-going skillet to make *Liver-Vegetable Dutch Puff* with its egg-pastry crust.

on the range

easy chicken curry

Assembling time: 15 minutes
Cooking time: 30 minutes

1 2½- to 3-pound broiler-
    fryer chicken, cut up
2 tablespoons cooking oil
¼ cup chopped onion
3 to 4 teaspoons curry
    powder
½ of a 21-ounce can apple
    pie filling
⅓ cup tomato juice
¼ teaspoon salt
⅓ cup milk
    Hot cooked rice

Season chicken with a little salt and pepper. In a 12-inch skillet brown the chicken in hot oil. Remove chicken from skillet; set aside. Add onion and curry to skillet; cook till onion is tender but not brown. Cut up apple pie filling into small pieces; add to skillet.

   Stir in tomato juice and salt. Return chicken to skillet. Cook, covered, over low heat for 25 to 30 minutes or till chicken is tender. Remove chicken to platter; keep warm. Add milk to apple mixture; bring just to boiling. Serve sauce over chicken and hot cooked rice. Makes 4 to 6 servings.

spicy chicken drumsticks

Assembling time: 20 minutes
Cooking time: 25 minutes

2 tablespoons all-purpose
    flour
¼ teaspoon salt
    Dash pepper
8 chicken drumsticks
1 tablespoon cooking oil
1 7½-ounce can tomatoes,
    cut up
1 tablespoon minced dried
    onion
2 teaspoons
    Worcestershire sauce
1 teaspoon sugar
½ teaspoon salt

In paper or plastic bag combine flour, ¼ teaspoon salt, and pepper. Add drumsticks, 2 or 3 at a time, and shake to coat. In 10-inch skillet brown chicken in hot oil. Drain off fat. Add *undrained* tomatoes, dried onion, Worcestershire sauce, sugar, and ½ teaspoon salt. Bring to boiling. Cover and simmer about 25 minutes or till chicken is tender. Remove chicken to serving platter. Spoon sauce over chicken. Makes 4 servings.

chicken breasts in herbed tomato sauce

Assembling time: 15 minutes
Cooking time: 25 minutes

3 whole medium chicken
    breasts, skinned,
    halved lengthwise, and
    boned
2 tablespoons butter *or*
    margarine
1 10¾-ounce can
    condensed tomato
    soup
¼ cup water
1 teaspoon minced dried
    onion
1 teaspoon dried basil,
    crushed
½ teaspoon dried oregano,
    crushed
    Dash salt
    Dash pepper
½ cup dairy sour cream
    Hot cooked noodles

In 10-inch skillet slowly brown chicken in butter or margarine about 10 minutes. Add tomato soup, water, dried onion, basil, oregano, salt, and pepper. Cover and simmer about 20 minutes or till chicken is tender. Remove chicken to platter; keep warm. Blend some pan juices into sour cream. Return to skillet. Cook and stir till heated through.

   Arrange chicken atop noodles; spoon some sauce atop; pass remainder. Makes 6 servings.

chicken cutlets

Assembling time: 10 minutes
Cooking time: 15 minutes

- **1 whole medium chicken breast, skinned, halved lengthwise, and boned**
- **1 large carrot, thinly sliced**
- **1 small onion, sliced and separated into rings**
- **1 small clove garlic, minced**
- **¼ teaspoon dried thyme, crushed**
- **2 tablespoons butter *or* margarine**

Pound chicken breast to ¼-inch thickness. In 8-inch skillet cook carrot, onion, garlic, and thyme in butter or margarine about 5 minutes or till tender but not brown. Push vegetables to edge of skillet. Add chicken pieces to skillet; cook over medium-high heat about 3 minutes on each side. To serve, top each chicken piece with some of the vegetables. Season with salt and pepper. Makes 2 servings.

chicken stroganoff

Assembling time: 10 minutes
Cooking time: 15 minutes

- **2 whole medium chicken breasts, skinned, halved lengthwise, and boned**
- **2 tablespoons cooking oil**
- **1 10¾-ounce can condensed cream of chicken soup**
- **1 6-ounce can sliced mushrooms, drained**
- **2 tablespoons chopped pimiento**
- **1 tablespoon dried parsley flakes**
- **⅛ teaspoon minced dried garlic**
- **½ cup sour cream with French onion**
- **1 tablespoon all-purpose flour**
  Hot cooked noodles

Cut chicken breasts into bite-size strips. In 10-inch skillet cook and stir chicken in hot oil about 5 minutes or till chicken is tender. Drain off excess fat. Add soup, mushrooms, pimiento, dried parsley, and dried garlic. Heat through. Combine sour cream and flour; stir into chicken mixture. Heat through; do not boil. Serve over noodles. Makes 4 servings.

raisin-sauced chicken

Assembling time: 10 minutes
Cooking time: 30 minutes

- **1 7½-ounce can tomatoes, cut up**
- **¼ cup raisins**
- **1 teaspoon instant chicken bouillon granules**
- **⅛ teaspoon allspice**
- **2 whole medium chicken breasts, skinned, halved lengthwise, and boned**
- **1 3-ounce package cream cheese with chives, cubed**
- **2 tablespoons milk**
  Hot cooked noodles

In medium skillet combine *un-drained* tomatoes, raisins, bouillon granules, and allspice. Bring to boiling; reduce heat. Add chicken. Cover and simmer for 25 to 30 minutes or till chicken is tender. Remove chicken; keep warm. Add cream cheese to skillet juices; stir with wire wisk till melted. Stir in milk. Arrange chicken on hot cooked noodles; spoon sauce atop. Makes 4 servings.

27

on the range

wine-poached fish

Assembling time: 20 minutes
Cooking time: 25 minutes

1 16-ounce package frozen fish fillets
½ cup water
¼ cup dry white wine
1 large carrot, thinly bias sliced
2 tablespoons sliced green onion
1 teaspoon dried parsley flakes
½ teaspoon instant chicken bouillon granules
¼ teaspoon dried tarragon, crushed
¼ teaspoon salt
   Dash pepper
¼ cup milk
2 teaspoons cornstarch

Let fish stand at room temperature for 20 minutes; cut crosswise into 4 equal-sized portions. Meanwhile, grease a 10-inch skillet. In skillet combine water, wine, carrot, onion, parsley flakes, bouillon granules, tarragon, salt, and pepper. Add fish. Bring to boiling; reduce heat. Cover and simmer about 20 minutes or till fish flakes easily when tested with a fork. Remove fish to serving platter; keep warm.

Blend milk and cornstarch; add to skillet mixture. Cook and stir till thickened and bubbly. Cook and stir 1 to 2 minutes more. Pour over fish. Makes 4 servings.

seafood chowder

Assembling time: 10 minutes
Cooking time: 20 minutes

1 16-ounce package frozen fish fillets
2 slices bacon, cut up
¼ cup chopped onion
3 tablespoons all-purpose flour
2½ cups milk
½ of an 8-ounce package frozen peeled and deveined shrimp
1 8-ounce can whole kernel corn, drained
1 2½-ounce jar sliced mushrooms, drained
1 2-ounce jar sliced pimiento, drained
1 tablespoon dried parsley flakes
2 teaspoons instant chicken bouillon granules

Let fish stand at room temperature about 20 minutes. Meanwhile, in 3-quart saucepan cook bacon till crisp. Remove bacon, reserving drippings. Cook onion in drippings till tender. Stir flour, ½ teaspoon *salt,* and ⅛ teaspoon *pepper* into bacon drippings. Add milk. Cook and stir till thickened and bubbly.

Cut fish into 1-inch cubes. Add fish, bacon, shrimp, corn, mushrooms, pimiento, parsley, and bouillon. Simmer 15 to 20 minutes or till fish flakes easily. Serves 6.

peppery fish stir-fry

Pictured on the cover

Assembling time: 30 minutes
Cooking time: 10 minutes

1 16-ounce package frozen fish fillets
1 15¼-ounce can pineapple chunks (juice pack)
1 tablespoon cornstarch
¼ cup soy sauce
¼ teaspoon crushed red pepper
2 tablespoons cooking oil
2 small red *or* green sweet peppers, cut into ¾-inch pieces
½ cup slivered almonds *or* peanuts
   Hot cooked rice

Let fish stand at room temperature for 20 minutes. Meanwhile, drain pineapple, reserving juice; set pineapple chunks aside. In small bowl blend reserved pineapple juice and cornstarch. Stir in soy sauce and red pepper. Set aside. Cut fish into 1-inch pieces.

In wok or large skillet stir-fry fish pieces in hot oil for 3 minutes; remove from wok. Stir-fry sweet pepper 1 minute; add almonds or peanuts. Stir-fry 1 minute more. Add pineapple juice mixture; cook and stir till bubbly. Stir in fish pieces and pineapple. Cover; heat 1 minute. Serve over rice. Serves 4.

Serve *Peppery Fish Stir-Fry* on a bed of cooked rice. Use quick-cooking rice to save time.

on
the range

saucy tuna and vegetables

Total time: 20 minutes

  3 tablespoons butter *or* margarine
  3 tablespoons all-purpose flour
1½ cups milk
  1 tablespoon minced dried onion
  1 3-ounce package cream cheese, cubed
  1 6½-ounce can tuna, drained and coarsely flaked, *or* one 6¾-ounce can chunk-style chicken, drained
  1 10-ounce package frozen peas
  2 tablespoons soy sauce
    Chow mein noodles

In saucepan melt butter or margarine. Stir in flour till smooth. Add milk and minced dried onion. Cook and stir till thickened and bubbly. Cook and stir 1 to 2 minutes more. Stir in cream cheese till melted. Add tuna or chicken, frozen peas, and soy sauce; heat through. Serve over chow mein noodles. Makes 4 servings.

salmon patties

Assembling time: 10 minutes
Cooking time: 10 minutes

  1 beaten egg
  2 tablespoons fine dry seasoned bread crumbs
  2 tablespoons orange juice
  1 teaspoon minced dried onion
  ⅛ teaspoon pepper
  1 7¾-ounce can salmon, drained
  3 tablespoons fine dry seasoned bread crumbs
  2 tablespoons cooking oil
  2 tablespoons dairy sour cream

In bowl combine egg, 2 tablespoons bread crumbs, orange juice, dried onion, and pepper. Remove bones and skin from salmon; flake meat. Add salmon; mix well. Shape into two patties. Coat with the 3 tablespoons bread crumbs.

  In medium skillet heat oil. Cook patties over medium-low heat about 5 minutes per side or till browned. To serve, top each patty with a dollop of sour cream. Makes 2 servings.

spaghetti with red clam sauce

Assembling time: 10 minutes
Cooking time: 25 minutes

  1 16-ounce can tomatoes, cut up
  1 6-ounce can tomato paste
  ⅓ cup dry red wine
  2 tablespoons dried parsley flakes
  1 tablespoon minced dried onion
  1 tablespoon sugar
  1 teaspoon garlic powder
  ½ teaspoon salt
  ½ teaspoon dried basil, crushed
  ¼ teaspoon dried oregano, crushed
    Dash pepper
  2 7½-ounce cans minced clams
    Hot cooked spaghetti

In large saucepan combine *undrained* tomatoes, tomato paste, wine, parsley flakes, dried onion, sugar, garlic powder, salt, basil, oregano, and pepper. Bring to boiling. Simmer, uncovered, 15 minutes, stirring occasionally. Add *undrained* clams. Simmer 5 minutes more. Serve over hot cooked spaghetti. Makes 4 servings.

corn frittata

Assembling time: 10 minutes
Cooking time: 10 minutes

- **2 tablespoons butter *or* margarine**
- **6 beaten eggs**
- **1 8¾-ounce can whole kernel corn, drained**
- **2 tablespoons chopped pimiento**
- **1 teaspoon minced dried onion**
- **½ teaspoon salt**
- **⅛ teaspoon pepper**
- **¼ cup sliced pitted ripe olives**

In a 10-inch oven-going skillet melt the butter or margarine. In mixing bowl combine eggs, corn, pimiento, dried onion, salt, and pepper. Pour mixture into skillet. Cook over medium-low heat.

As eggs set, run a spatula around edge of skillet, lifting egg mixture to allow uncooked portion to flow underneath. Continue cooking and lifting edges till mixture is almost set (surface will be moist).

Place skillet under the broiler 5 inches from heat. Broil for 1 to 2 minutes or just till top is set. Sprinkle sliced olives atop. Loosen bottom of frittata and slide out onto plate. Cut into wedges. Makes 3 servings.

hash brown omelet

Assembling time: 5 minutes
Cooking time: 10 minutes

- **1 cup frozen loose-pack hash brown potatoes, partially thawed**
- **2 tablespoons finely chopped onion**
- **2 tablespoons snipped parsley**
- **2 tablespoons butter *or* margarine**
- **¼ teaspoon salt**
  Dash pepper
- **4 beaten eggs**

In an 8-inch skillet cook potatoes, onion, and parsley in butter or margarine over medium heat for 5 minutes; sprinkle with the salt and pepper. Pour in eggs; cook over medium heat.

As eggs set, run a spatula around edge of skillet, lifting the eggs to allow uncooked portion to flow underneath. When eggs are set but still shiny, remove from heat. Turn out onto serving platter. Makes 2 servings.

easy eggs benedict

Total time: 45 minutes

- **6 frozen patty shells**
- **1 1¾-ounce envelope hollandaise sauce mix**
- **1 cup milk**
- **4 beaten eggs**
- **⅛ teaspoon salt**
  Dash pepper
- **2 tablespoons butter *or* margarine**
- **3 slices Canadian-style bacon, cut up**
- **1 to 2 tablespoons sliced green onion**

Bake patty shells according to package directions. Meanwhile, in small saucepan stir together hollandaise sauce mix and 1 cup milk. Cook and stir till thickened and bubbly; keep warm.

Combine eggs, ⅓ cup of the prepared hollandaise sauce, the salt, and pepper. In medium skillet melt butter; pour in egg mixture. To scramble eggs, cook without stirring till mixture just begins to set. Lift and fold the partially cooked eggs so the uncooked portion flows underneath.

Stir in bacon pieces. Continue cooking for 3 to 5 minutes or till eggs are cooked. Remove from heat. Spoon egg-bacon mixture into patty shells. Top each with hollandaise sauce; garnish with green onion. Serves 3.

31

under the broiler

harvest pork kebabs

Assembling time: 20 minutes
Cooking time: 25 minutes

**1 medium yellow
   crookneck squash, cut
   into 1-inch pieces
1 pound boneless pork, cut
   into 1-inch cubes
2 medium cooking apples,
   cored and each cut into
   eighths
½ of a 6-ounce can (⅓ cup)
   frozen apple juice
   concentrate, thawed
1 tablespoon honey
1 teaspoon cornstarch
¼ teaspoon ground allspice**

Thread squash, pork, and
apple slices alternately on 8
skewers, piercing squash
through its skin.

   In saucepan combine apple
juice concentrate, honey, cornstarch, and allspice; cook and
stir till thickened and bubbly.
Cook and stir 1 to 2 minutes
more. Place kebabs on rack of
unheated broiler pan. Broil 3
to 4 inches from heat for 8 to
10 minutes. Brush with sauce;
turn kebabs. Broil 8 to 10 minutes more or till pork is done.
Brush again with sauce just
before serving. Makes 4
servings.

peanutty pork chops

Assembling time: 15 minutes
Cooking time: 30 minutes

**½ cup herb-seasoned
   stuffing croutons
¼ cup chopped peanuts
2 tablespoons chopped
   green pepper
3 tablespoons butter *or*
   margarine, melted
2 teaspoons dry white wine
   or water
4 pork loin rib chops, cut
   1 inch thick**

In bowl combine croutons,
peanuts, and green pepper.
Combine melted butter or margarine and wine or water;
sprinkle over crouton mixture
and toss. Using a sharp knife,
cut a pocket in each chop by
cutting a 1½- to 2-inch-long
slit in the fatty side of the
chop. Then, insert the knife
into the slit and draw knife's
tip side to side to form a
larger pocket inside the chop,
cutting almost to bone edge.
Try not to make the first slit
any larger so closing the chop
will be easier. Season the cavity with salt and pepper.

   Stuff chops with crouton
mixture; secure with wooden
picks. Place on rack of unheated broiler pan. Broil 5
inches from heat about 30
minutes *total time*, turning
once. Makes 4 servings.

tangy pork steaks

Assembling time: 20 minutes
Cooking time: 20 minutes

**⅓ cup cooking oil
3 tablespoons soy sauce
2 tablespoons wine
   vinegar
1 tablespoon lemon juice
1 tablespoon
   Worcestershire sauce
1½ teaspoons dry mustard
1 small clove garlic,
   crushed
½ teaspoon pepper
¼ teaspoon salt
4 pork blade steaks, cut
   ½ inch thick**

Combine oil, soy sauce, wine
vinegar, lemon juice, Worcestershire sauce, dry mustard,
garlic, pepper, and salt; mix
well. Place steaks in shallow
baking dish; pour marinade
over steaks. Let stand 15 minutes at room temperature *or* 3
to 4 hours in refrigerator, turning steaks once. Drain, reserving marinade.

   Place steaks on rack of unheated broiler pan. Broil 3
inches from heat for 8 to 10
minutes. Brush with marinade.
Turn steaks; broil 8 to 10 minutes more, brushing with marinade after 5 minutes. Brush
with marinade just before
serving. Makes 4 servings.

cherry-sauced ham slice

Total time: 20 minutes

- 1 **2-pound fully cooked ham slice, cut 1 inch thick**
- 1 **16-ounce can pitted dark sweet cherries**
- 1 **tablespoon cornstarch**
- ½ **teaspoon ground cinnamon**
- ¼ **teaspoon ground cloves**
- 3 **tablespoons dry white wine**
- ½ **teaspoon finely shredded lemon peel**
- 1 **tablespoon lemon juice**
- ⅓ **cup coarsely chopped walnuts**

Slash fat edge of ham slice. Place on rack of unheated broiler pan. Broil ham 3 inches from heat for 7 to 8 minutes. Turn; broil 7 to 8 minutes more or till heated through.

Meanwhile, for sauce, drain cherries, reserving syrup. In medium saucepan combine cornstarch, cinnamon, and cloves. Stir in reserved syrup, wine, lemon peel, and lemon juice. Cook and stir till thickened and bubbly. Cook and stir 1 to 2 minutes more. Stir in cherries and nuts; heat through. Spoon some sauce over ham slice; pass remainder. Makes 8 servings.

glazed lamb chops

Assembling time: 5 minutes
Cooking time: 11 minutes

- 4 **lamb loin** *or* **shoulder chops, cut ¾ inch thick**
- ¼ **cup apple jelly**
- ¼ **cup chopped pecans**
- 1 **tablespoon lemon juice**
- ¼ **teaspoon ground cinnamon**

Place lamb chops on rack of unheated broiler pan. Broil 3 to 4 inches from heat for 5 minutes. Season chops with salt and pepper. Turn; broil chops 3 to 5 minutes more.

Meanwhile, combine jelly, pecans, lemon juice, and cinnamon. Spread jelly mixture over chops; broil 1 minute more. Makes 4 servings.
Note: A lamb loin chop is identified by the T-shaped backbone, loin eye muscle, and smaller tenderloin muscle. A lamb shoulder chop has either a blade or arm bone.

spiced lamb kebabs

Assembling time: 35 minutes
Cooking time: 10 minutes

- ½ **cup dry white wine**
- 2 **tablespoons cooking oil**
- 2 **teaspoons ground coriander**
- 1 **teaspoon ground ginger**
- ½ **teaspoon salt**
- ¼ **teaspoon ground cinnamon**
- ¼ **teaspoon ground cloves**
- 1 **pound boneless lamb, cut into 1-inch cubes**
- 16 **fresh large mushrooms**
- 1 **medium zucchini, cut into ½-inch slices**
- 1 **8-ounce carton plain yogurt**

In bowl combine wine, oil, coriander, ginger, salt, cinnamon, cloves, and ⅛ teaspoon *pepper*. Remove 2 tablespoons of the marinade; set aside. Add lamb cubes to the remaining marinade; let stand at room temperature for 15 minutes.

Drain lamb, reserving marinade. Thread lamb, mushrooms, and zucchini alternately on skewers; brush with marinade. Place on rack of unheated broiler pan. Broil 4 inches from heat for 5 to 6 minutes. Turn and brush again with marinade. Broil 5 to 6 minutes more or till desired doneness. Meanwhile, combine reserved marinade and yogurt; serve with kebabs. Makes 4 servings.

33

under the broiler

quick london broil

Assembling time: 25 minutes
Cooking time: 10 minutes

**1 1- to 1¼-pound beef flank
   steak**
¼ cup cooking oil
3 tablespoons soy sauce
1 tablespoon dry sherry
1 teaspoon vinegar
¼ teaspoon dry mustard
   Dash pepper
   Dash garlic powder

Score steak diagonally on both
sides. Place steak in shallow
baking dish. Combine oil, soy
sauce, dry sherry, vinegar, dry
mustard, pepper, and garlic
powder; pour over steak. Let
stand at room temperature for
15 minutes, turning steak
once.
  Remove steak from mari-
nade, reserving marinade.
Place steak on rack of unheated broiler pan. Broil 3
inches from heat for 4 to 5
minutes. Turn; brush with
marinade.
  Broil 4 to 5 minutes more
for medium-rare doneness. To
serve, brush steak with marinade and carve into very thin
slices diagonally across the
grain. Makes 4 or 5 servings.

teriyaki orange burgers

Assembling time: 15 minutes
Cooking time: 15 minutes

1½ pounds ground beef
**1 1⅝-ounce envelope
   teriyaki sauce mix**
**¼ cup water chestnuts,
   drained and chopped**
1 orange
¼ cup water
**1 teaspoon sesame seed,
   toasted**

In bowl combine ground beef,
half of the dry sauce mix, and
the water chestnuts. Shape
into patties ½ inch thick. Place
patties on rack of unheated
broiler pan. Broil 3 inches from
heat, turning once, till desired
doneness (allow about 10 minutes total time for medium
doneness).
  Peel orange. Cut into 6
slices. Place an orange slice
atop each patty; broil 1 minute
more. Combine remaining
sauce mix with ¼ cup water.
Stir in sesame seed; spoon
over hot patties. Makes 6
servings.

steak with chutney

Assembling time: 15 minutes
Cooking time: 15 minutes

**1 2½-pound beef sirloin
   steak, cut 1 inch thick**
**1 9-ounce jar (⅔ cup)
   chutney**
**2 tablespoons butter *or*
   margarine**
2 tablespoons lemon juice
**2 to 3 teaspoons curry
   powder**
**1 small red *or* green sweet
   pepper, cut into rings**

Slash fat edges of meat to
prevent curling. In small
saucepan combine chutney,
butter or margarine, lemon
juice, and curry powder; heat
and stir till butter melts and
mixture bubbles.
  Place steak on rack of unheated broiler pan. Broil 3
inches from heat for 5 to 7
minutes. Brush meat with
some of the chutney mixture.
Turn; continue broiling 5 to 7
minutes more or till desired
doneness. Add pepper rings to
remaining sauce; heat
through. Spoon over steak.
Makes 4 servings.
Note: Next time try this recipe
using pork blade steaks or
lamb sirloin chops.

Serve juicy broiled *Steak with
Chutney* with *Curried Risotto*
(see recipe, page 81).

BROILING MEAT

Use the chart below as a guide for broiling the desired cut of meat. (Before broiling beef steaks or lamb chops, slash the fat edge to keep meat from curling.) Place meat on rack of unheated broiler pan. Broil according to the distance from heat and the time specified in the chart. Broil about half the time indicated for desired doneness. Season; turn. Broil till desired doneness. Season again. Serve broiled meat with one of the easy sauces below.

cut of meat	thickness	distance from heat	broiling time (total minutes)
BEEF STEAKS (choose from beef T-bone, porterhouse, top loin, sirloin, or tenderloin)	1 inch	3 inches	8-10 (rare) 12-14 (medium) 18-20 (well-done)
	1½ inches	3 inches	14-16 (rare) 18-20 (medium) 25-30 (well-done)
	2 inches	4-5 inches	20-25 (rare) 30-35 (medium) 40-45 (well-done)
HAMBURGERS (use one pound of ground beef to shape into four patties)	½ inch	3 inches	8 (rare) 10 (medium) 12 (well-done)
PORK CHOPS AND STEAKS pork rib or pork loin chops	¾-1 inch	3-4 inches	20-25 (well-done)
pork shoulder steaks	½-¾ inch	3-4 inches	20-22 (well-done)
LAMB CHOPS (choose from rib, loin, or leg sirloin chops)	¾-1 inch	3 inches	10-12 (medium) 14-16 (well-done)

quick soup sauce

In saucepan combine one 10¾-ounce can *condensed cream of celery or cream of mushroom soup,* ⅓ cup *milk,* 1 tablespoon *lemon juice,* 1 teaspoon *minced dried onion,* and ¼ teaspoon *ground sage;* heat through. Serve with lamb or poultry. Makes 1½ cups.

chilly yogurt sauce

Combine one 8-ounce container *plain yogurt,* 3 tablespoons *bottled barbecue sauce,* and ¼ teaspoon dried *tarragon,* crushed. Chill 3 hours. Serve with beef, pork, or lamb. Makes about 1 cup.

chop-chop

Combine ½ cup chopped *green pepper,* ½ cup chopped *onion,* and ½ cup *chili sauce.* Cover and chill. Serve with burgers or frankfurters. Makes 1½ cups.

barbecue sauce

Combine one 14-ounce bottle *hot-style catsup,* 3 tablespoons *vinegar,* 2 teaspoons *celery seed,* and 1 clove *garlic,* halved. Cover; chill. Remove garlic. Brush burgers or beef during the last 5 minutes of broiling. Makes about 1½ cups.

snappy citrus sauce

In saucepan combine ½ cup *orange marmalade,* ¼ cup *raisins,* and 1 tablespoon *lemon juice.* Heat slowly till marmalade is melted, stirring occasionally. Serve with pork, lamb, or poultry. Makes ⅔ cup.

herbed butter log

Combine: 6 tablespoons softened *butter;* 1 teaspoon *lemon juice;* ½ teaspoon dried *tarragon,* crushed; and ⅛ teaspoon *garlic powder.* Shape into a 4-inch-long log on waxed paper. Chill in refrigerator or freezer till firm. Slice butter log. Serve on broiled steaks or burgers.

under
the broiler

broiled orange chicken

Pictured on pages 8 and 9

Assembling time: 5 minutes
Cooking time: 35 minutes

1 2½- to 3-pound broiler-fryer chicken, cut up
Cooking oil
½ cup bottled barbecue sauce
½ cup orange marmalade, plum preserves, *or* pineapple preserves

Brush chicken pieces with oil; season with salt and pepper. Place chicken, skin side down, on rack of unheated broiler pan. Broil 5 to 6 inches from heat about 20 minutes. Turn; broil about 10 minutes more. Meanwhile, for sauce, in saucepan combine barbecue sauce and marmalade or preserves. Brush chicken pieces with sauce; broil about 5 minutes more or till tender.

Meanwhile, heat sauce through. To serve, brush chicken with sauce and pass remainder. Garnish chicken with an orange slice, lemon slice, and curly endive, if desired. Makes 6 servings.

chili drumsticks on rice

Assembling time: 10 minutes
Cooking time: 30 minutes

½ of a 6-ounce can (⅓ cup) frozen orange juice concentrate, thawed
2 tablespoons cooking oil
2 teaspoons chili powder
¼ teaspoon onion powder
8 chicken legs (about ¾ pound)
1 11-ounce package frozen rice with bell peppers and parsley

For sauce, in bowl combine orange juice concentrate, cooking oil, chili powder, and onion powder. Place chicken on rack of unheated broiler pan. Broil 5 to 6 inches from heat about 25 minutes, turning once. Brush with sauce. Broil for 2 to 3 minutes more. Turn, brush with sauce. Broil 2 to 3 minutes more.

Meanwhile, prepare rice according to package directions. To serve, place broiled chicken atop rice. Pass remaining sauce. Makes 4 servings.
Note: To quick thaw an unopened can of frozen juice concentrate, let it sit in a bowl of hot water a few minutes.

cheddar chicken rolls

Assembling time: 15 minutes
Cooking time: 30 minutes

1 4-ounce package (1 cup) shredded sharp cheddar cheese
1 tablespoon water
1 teaspoon minced dried onion
⅛ teaspoon dried tarragon, crushed
4 whole medium chicken breasts, skinned, halved lengthwise, and boned
3 tablespoons butter *or* margarine, melted

Combine cheese, water, dried onion, and tarragon; set aside. Place chicken breasts, boned side up, between two pieces of clear plastic wrap. Pound with flat side of meat mallet to ⅛-inch thickness. Remove plastic wrap; season both sides of chicken with salt and pepper.

Divide cheese mixture among chicken breasts, spooning onto each chicken piece. Fold in sides and roll up jelly-roll style. Be sure the folded sides are inside the roll. Skewer closed with wooden picks. Place chicken rolls on baking sheet. Brush chicken with melted butter or margarine. Broil 5 to 6 inches from heat about 15 minutes. Turn and brush with butter; broil 15 minutes more. Serves 4.

37

under
the broiler

marinated chicken

Assembling time: 25 minutes
Cooking time: 8 minutes

- **4 whole medium chicken breasts, skinned, halved lengthwise, and boned**
- **⅓ cup creamy Italian *or* onion salad dressing**
- **2 tablespoons dry white wine**

Place chicken breasts between 2 pieces of clear plastic wrap. Pound with flat side of meat mallet to ¼-inch thickness.

Remove wrap; place chicken in shallow dish. Combine salad dressing and wine; pour over chicken. Cover; marinate at room temperature 20 minutes. Drain; reserve marinade.

Place chicken on rack of unheated broiler pan. Broil 3 to 4 inches from heat for 3 to 4 minutes per side, brushing with reserved marinade occasionally. Makes 8 servings.

SHORTCUT TIP: CHICKEN BREASTS

When preparing a recipe that calls for boned chicken breasts, save time by buying chicken breasts that are already skinned, halved lengthwise, and boned.

curried turkey burgers

Assembling time: 15 minutes
Cooking time: 16 minutes

- **1 1¼-ounce envelope sour cream sauce mix**
- **¾ teaspoon curry powder**
- **1 beaten egg**
- **⅓ cup quick-cooking rolled oats**
- **2 tablespoons snipped chives**
- **½ teaspoon salt**
  Dash pepper
- **1½ pounds ground raw turkey**
- **6 kaiser rolls (optional)**

Prepare sour cream sauce mix according to package directions. Stir in curry powder. Keep warm. In bowl stir together ⅓ cup of the curry sauce, the beaten egg, rolled oats, chives, salt, and pepper; add ground turkey and mix well. Shape into six 1-inch-thick patties. Place patties on rack of unheated broiler pan. Broil 3 inches from heat, turning once, for 14 to 16 minutes *total time* or till well-done. Spoon remaining sauce over hot patties. Serve on split kaiser rolls, if desired. Makes 6 servings.

fruited fish fillets

Pictured on pages 8 and 9

Assembling time: 20 minutes
Cooking time: 25 minutes

- **2 16-ounce packages frozen fish fillets**
- **¼ cup butter *or* margarine, melted**
- **1 11-ounce can mandarin orange sections**
- **2 tablespoons dry white wine**
- **2 teaspoons cornstarch**
- **⅓ cup raisins**
- **1 tablespoon snipped parsley**

Allow frozen fish to stand at room temperature for 15 minutes. Cut fish into 8 portions; place on unheated rack of broiler pan. Brush with some of the melted butter. Season.

Broil 4 inches from heat till fish flakes easily when tested with a fork. (Allow 20 to 24 minutes *total time* for each inch of thickness, turning halfway through cooking time. After turning, brush again with melted butter.) Meanwhile, drain mandarin orange sections, reserving juice. In saucepan combine reserved juice, wine, and cornstarch. Cook and stir till thickened and bubbly. Cook and stir 1 to 2 minutes more. Stir in mandarin orange sections, raisins, and parsley. Keep warm. Serve fish with fruit mixture. Garnish with parsley, if desired. Serves 8.

herbed salmon steaks

Assembling time: 5 minutes
Cooking time: 20 minutes

**3 tablespoons butter *or*
    margarine, melted**
2 teaspoons lemon juice
**1 teaspoon dried tarragon,
    crushed**
**4 frozen salmon steaks, cut
    1 inch thick (about 1½
    pounds)**
**½ of a 2-ounce envelope (3
    tablespoons) seasoned
    coating mix for fish**
**1 teaspoon snipped parsley
    Lemon wedges**

Stir together butter or margarine, lemon juice, and tarragon.
Brush frozen fish steaks with
tarragon butter. Place fish on
rack of unheated broiler pan.
Broil 3 to 4 inches from heat
about 9 minutes. Brush with
butter; turn and brush again.
Broil about 9 minutes more or
till almost done. Sprinkle coating mix atop steaks. Broil
about 2 minutes or till
browned. To serve, sprinkle
with parsley, and garnish serving platter with lemon wedges.
Makes 4 servings.
Note: If using thawed salmon
steaks, broil for 4 to 5 minutes
on each side before adding
coating mix. Continue as
directed.

savory shrimp broil

Assembling time: 35 minutes
Cooking time: 8 minutes

**12 ounces fresh *or* frozen
    shelled shrimp**
⅓ cup cooking oil
¼ cup dry white wine
¼ cup soy sauce
1 clove garlic, minced
¼ teaspoon ground ginger
**¼ teaspoon paprika
    Dash pepper**

If frozen, thaw shrimp under
cold, running water. In bowl
combine cooking oil, wine, soy
sauce, garlic, ginger, paprika,
and pepper. Add shrimp; cover
and let stand at room temperature for 15 minutes.
    Drain shrimp, reserving mar-
inade; thread shrimp on skewers. Broil 4 to 5 inches from
heat for 4 minutes, basting occasionally with marinade. Turn
and broil for 2 to 4 minutes
more or till shrimp are done.
Makes 4 servings.

scallop kebabs

Assembling time: 20 minutes
Cooking time: 12 minutes

**1 pound fresh *or* frozen
    scallops**
**2 green peppers, cut into
    1-inch pieces**
**⅓ cup unsweetened
    pineapple juice**
**2 tablespoons butter *or*
    margarine, melted**
1 teaspoon dried dillweed

Place frozen scallops in a colander; run cold water over
scallops about 5 minutes or till
partially thawed. Halve any
large scallops. Thread scallops
and green pepper alternately
on six skewers.
    In bowl combine pineapple
juice, butter or margarine, and
dillweed. Brush kebabs with
juice mixture. Place kebabs on
rack of unheated broiler pan.
Broil 3 to 4 inches from heat
for 4 to 6 minutes. Turn kebabs carefully; brush with juice
mixture. Broil for 4 to 6 minutes more or till scallops are
opaque. Brush with juice mixture just before serving.
Makes 6 servings.

39

salads and sandwiches

hot pizza salad

Total time: 25 minutes

¾ **pound bulk pork sausage**
   or **bulk sweet Italian**
   sausage
1 **8-ounce can pizza sauce**
   Few dashes bottled hot
   pepper sauce (optional)
4 **cups torn lettuce**
1 **medium tomato, cut into**
   wedges
½ **cup sliced pitted ripe**
   olives
¼ **cup chopped green**
   pepper
1 **4-ounce package (1 cup)**
   shredded mozzarella
   cheese
   Ripe olives (optional)

In skillet cook sausage till browned; drain off fat. Stir in pizza sauce and hot pepper sauce, if desired. Cover; simmer about 5 minutes.

Meanwhile, in salad bowl combine lettuce, tomato, sliced olives, green pepper, and *half* the cheese; toss. Spoon hot meat mixture over salad. Top with remaining cheese. Garnish with olives, if desired. Toss again to serve. Makes 4 servings.

spinach-sausage salad

Total time: 25 minutes

4 **cups torn spinach**
1 **cup shredded carrot**
4 **ounces assorted dry and**
   semidry sausages, cut
   into strips (1 cup)
1 **cup shredded cheddar**
   cheese (4 ounces)
1 **cup sliced cucumber**
8 **cherry tomatoes**
4 **slices Melba toast,**
   broken
4 **slices bacon**
¼ **cup vinegar**
1 **teaspoon Worcestershire**
   sauce

In large salad bowl toss together spinach and shredded carrot. Arrange sausage, cheese, cucumber, cherry tomatoes, and Melba toast atop. In skillet cook bacon till crisp; remove and drain bacon, reservings drippings.

Crumble bacon and sprinkle on salad. In skillet stir together bacon drippings, vinegar, and Worcestershire sauce; heat through. Pour hot dressing over salad. Toss. Makes 4 servings.

kiwi shrimp salad

Total time: 25 minutes

6 **cups torn spinach** *or*
   other greens
1 **11-ounce can mandarin**
   orange sections, chilled
   and drained
2 **4½-ounce cans large**
   shrimp, chilled,
   drained, and rinsed
2 **kiwi fruits, peeled and**
   sliced
¼ **cup sliced almonds**
½ **cup dairy sour cream**
¼ **cup peach nectar**
¼ **teaspoon finely shredded**
   orange peel
   Dash salt

In large bowl arrange the spinach, orange sections, shrimp, and kiwi fruit. Sprinkle with almonds. For dressing, in small bowl combine sour cream, peach nectar, orange peel, and salt; beat till smooth. Pour over salad and toss to coat. Makes 4 servings.

Fresh and colorful: *Kiwi Shrimp Salad* and *Cheesy Pita Bread Sandwiches* (see recipe, page 43).

salads and sandwiches

fruited turkey salad

Total time: 20 minutes

**4 cups torn mixed salad
  greens
1 11-ounce can mandarin
  orange sections,
  drained
2 5-ounce cans boned
  turkey *or* chicken,
  drained
1 cup seedless green
  grapes
¼ cup raisins
¼ cup salted peanuts
½ cup mayonnaise *or* salad
  dressing
½ cup lemon yogurt
½ teaspoon dried tarragon,
  crushed
¼ teaspoon paprika
  Dash ground red pepper**

In large salad bowl place salad greens. Arrange orange sections, turkey or chicken, grapes, raisins, and peanuts atop salad greens.

For dressing, stir together mayonnaise or salad dressing, yogurt, tarragon, paprika, and red pepper. If desired, cover and chill salad and dressing till serving time. Pass dressing with salad. Makes 4 servings.

luncheon meat- blue cheese salad

Total time: 25 minutes

**5 slices bacon
¼ cup salad oil
3 tablespoons vinegar
1 teaspoon Worcestershire
  sauce
½ teaspoon sugar
½ teaspoon dry mustard
6 cups torn lettuce
½ cup crumbled blue
  cheese (2 ounces)
2 tablespoons sliced green
  onion
1 12-ounce can luncheon
  meat, cut into strips**

In skillet cook bacon till crisp; drain. Crumble bacon and set aside.

In a screw-top jar combine salad oil, vinegar, Worcestershire sauce, sugar, and dry mustard. Shake to mix thoroughly.

In salad bowl combine lettuce, blue cheese, and onion. Arrange luncheon meat strips atop lettuce mixture. Sprinkle bacon over all. Shake dressing; pour over salad. Toss to coat. Makes 6 servings.

mexi-bean salad

Assembling time: 25 minutes
Chilling time: 1 hour

**1 15-ounce can garbanzo
  beans, drained
1 15-ounce can dark red
  kidney beans, drained
8 ounces Monterey Jack
  cheese *or* cheddar
  cheese, cubed
1 large tomato, chopped
  (1 cup)
2 tablespoons finely
  chopped onion
1 8-ounce container
  avocado dip
½ cup plain yogurt
1 teaspoon chili powder
¼ teaspoon salt
  Dash bottled hot pepper
  sauce
6 cups shredded cabbage
  Corn chips**

In large mixing bowl stir together garbanzo beans, kidney beans, cheese, tomato, and onion. Cover and chill about 1 hour. For dressing, in small bowl stir together avocado dip, yogurt, chili powder, salt, and hot pepper sauce. Cover and chill.

Pour dressing over bean-cheese mixture; toss lightly. To serve, place *1 cup* shredded cabbage on each of six individual salad plates. Spoon salad mixture over cabbage. Sprinkle corn chips atop. Makes 6 servings.

quick-baked reubens

Assembling time: 25 minutes
Cooking time: 10 minutes

2 packages (16) refrigerated crescent rolls
1 12-ounce can corned beef, flaked
1 cup sauerkraut relish, drained
1 tablespoon caraway seed
½ cup shredded Swiss cheese (2 ounces)
Milk

Unroll crescent roll dough; form into eight 6x3½-inch rectangles, pressing perforated edges together. Combine corned beef, sauerkraut relish, and caraway seed. Spoon about ¼ cup sauerkraut mixture onto half of each dough rectangle. Sprinkle cheese atop each. Fold over other half of dough; seal edges using tines of fork. Place on an ungreased baking sheet. Brush each with a little milk. Bake in a 425° oven about 10 minutes or till golden. Makes 8 sandwiches.

german potato salad sandwiches

Assembling time: 30 minutes
Cooking time: 6 minutes

2 eggs
8 fully cooked smoked sausage links (12 ounces)
1 16-ounce can German-style potato salad
4 English muffins, split and toasted
1 8-ounce container (1 cup) sour cream with French onion

To hard-cook eggs, place eggs in saucepan; cover with cold water. Bring to boiling; reduce heat to just below simmering. Cover and cook for 15 to 20 minutes. Cool eggs in *cold* water. Remove shells; chop eggs. Set aside.

Meanwhile, with sharp knife, slit each sausage crosswise into 7 sections, about ½ inch apart, cutting almost to, but not through other side. Shape each cut sausage into a circle; set aside. Spoon some potato salad atop each muffin half. Top with sausage circle. Spoon sour cream into center. Place on baking sheet; broil 3 to 4 inches from heat for 6 minutes. Top with chopped egg. Makes 4 servings.

cheesy pita bread sandwiches

Pictured on page 41

Total time: 20 minutes

1 3-ounce package cream cheese
1 8-ounce carton plain yogurt
2 tablespoons milk
1 teaspoon prepared mustard
1 12-ounce can luncheon meat, chopped
½ cup sliced pitted ripe olives
3 large pita bread rounds, halved
1 cup shredded cheddar cheese
1 large tomato, chopped
Alfalfa sprouts

Beat cream cheese till softened. Add yogurt, milk, and mustard; beat till smooth. Stir in luncheon meat and olives. Spoon mixture into halved pita bread rounds. Top each with shredded cheese, chopped tomato, and alfalfa sprouts. Serve immediately. Makes 6 servings.

43

salads and sandwiches

curried chicken salad sandwiches

Total time: 15 minutes

  1 5-ounce can boned
       chicken *or* turkey,
       drained
  ¼ cup chopped apple
  ¼ cup raisins
  3 tablespoons mayonnaise
       or salad dressing
  1 teaspoon lemon juice
  ½ teaspoon curry powder
       Butter *or* margarine
  4 slices whole wheat bread
  2 slices Swiss cheese
       (2 ounces)

Stir together chicken or turkey, apple, raisins, mayonnaise, lemon juice, and curry powder. Spread butter or margarine on one side of each bread slice.

  Spread chicken mixture on the buttered side of 2 bread slices; top with cheese. Top with remaining bread slices. Makes 2 servings.
Note: Serve the chicken filling on toasted bread, if desired.

sweet-sour sandwiches

Total time: 15 minutes

  1 2-ounce envelope sweet-
       sour sauce mix
  1 16-ounce can fancy mixed
       Chinese vegetables,
       drained
  2 5-ounce cans boned
       chicken *or* turkey
  1 tablespoon sliced green
       onion
  2 individual French rolls *or*
       English muffins
       Chow mein noodles

In medium saucepan prepare sweet-sour sauce mix according to package directions. Stir in vegetables, *undrained* chicken or turkey, and green onion; heat through.

  Split rolls; spoon chicken-vegetable mixture on rolls. Sprinkle chow mein noodles atop. Makes 4 servings.

tuna patty melt

Assembling time: 15 minutes
Cooking time: 9 minutes

  1 egg
  ⅔ cup quick-cooking rolled
       oats
  ½ cup sour cream with
       French onion
  1 stalk celery, chopped
       (½ cup)
  ¼ teaspoon celery seed
       Dash pepper
  2 6½-ounce cans tuna,
       drained and flaked
  2 tablespoons cooking oil
  ½ cup shredded American
       cheese
  6 slices dark rye bread,
       toasted *or* 6 hamburger
       buns, split and toasted

In bowl combine egg, rolled oats, sour cream, celery, celery seed, and pepper. Add tuna; mix well. Shape mixture into 6 patties. Heat oil in skillet.

  Cook tuna patties in hot oil, covered, about 8 minutes *total time* or till heated through, turning once. Sprinkle cheese atop each. Cook, covered, 1 minute more or till cheese is melted. Serve patties on rye bread or hamburger buns. Makes 6 servings.

hot salmon cups

Assembling time: 20 minutes
Cooking time: 18 minutes

1 15½-ounce can salmon
¾ cup shredded provolone
  cheese (3 ounces)
⅓ cup dairy sour cream
¼ cup chopped celery
3 tablespoons sweet pickle
  relish
2 teaspoons lemon juice
¼ teaspoon minced dried
  onion
1 package (10) refrigerated
  flaky biscuits

Drain salmon; flake fish, re-
moving skin and bones. In
bowl combine salmon, *half* of
the cheese, the sour cream,
celery, sweet pickle relish,
lemon juice, and minced dried
onion.

Separate biscuit dough into
10 biscuits. Place each biscuit
in an ungreased muffin pan;
press to cover bottom and
sides. Spoon about ¼ cup
salmon mixture into each biscuit cup.

Bake in 400° oven about 15
minutes or till crust is golden
brown. Sprinkle with remaining
cheese. Bake 2 to 3 minutes
more or till cheese is melted.
Remove from muffin pans and
serve warm. Makes 5 servings.

hollandaise-sauced fish sandwich

Total time: 25 minutes

1 8-ounce package (4)
  frozen breaded fish
  portions
1 1¾-ounce envelope
  hollandaise sauce mix
1 teaspoon minced dried
  onion
¼ teaspoon dried dillweed
1 cup shredded cabbage
4 bias-sliced French bread
  slices, cut ½ inch thick

Bake fish portions according
to package directions. Meanwhile, prepare hollandaise
sauce mix according to package directions; stir in onion
and dillweed.

Place ¼ cup shredded cab-
bage on each bread slice.
Place baked fish portions on
cabbage. Spoon sauce over
each sandwich. Makes 4
servings.

egg salad sandwich pizzas

Assembling time: 30 minutes
Cooking time: 5 minutes

4 eggs
1 4-ounce package (1 cup)
  shredded mozzarella
  cheese
½ of a 6-ounce can (⅓ cup)
  tomato paste
¼ cup mayonnaise *or* salad
  dressing
2 tablespoons finely
  chopped onion
¼ teaspoon salt
¼ teaspoon dried basil,
  crushed
¼ teaspoon dried oregano,
  crushed
  Dash garlic powder
  Dash pepper
4 English muffins, split and
  toasted

To hard-cook eggs, place eggs
in small saucepan; cover with
cold water. Bring to boiling; reduce heat to just below simmering. Cover and cook for 15
to 20 minutes. Cool eggs in
cold water. Meanwhile, in bowl
combine ½ *cup* of the cheese,
the tomato paste, mayonnaise,
onion, salt, basil, oregano, garlic
powder, and pepper.

Remove shells from eggs.
Chop eggs; stir into tomato
mixture. Spread mixture on
muffin halves, covering edges.
Broil 6 inches from heat for 3
minutes. Top with remaining
cheese and broil 2 minutes
more. Serves 4.

45

MAIN DISHES

Take advantage of those occasions when you have "extra" time—prepare frozen and cooked foods to use for more than one meal. This chapter shows you how frozen meat mixes and casseroles can be removed from the freezer when needed for a quick and easy meal.

Recipes for meatballs, stew mix, and ground meat mix that make more than one meal are in this chapter. Store these meat mixes in the freezer, ready to use in the accompanying recipes. Just add final ingredients to the frozen mix, cook and serve.

Freezer Casseroles are ideal for planning and preparing meals ahead. With our recipes you can bake one now, and freeze the extras. When needed, the frozen casserole is ready to bake without further preparation.

Cooked meat and poultry are also time-savers in meal preparation. Cook a beef roast or turkey, then freeze the chopped meat in small portions. Use the cooked meat or poultry in a recipe when you need a quick meal.

Pictured: *Biscuit-Topped Chicken Pies* (see recipe, page 63) are served as individual casseroles. *Wine-Sauced Meatballs*, an elegant main dish, starts with easy *Freezer Meatballs* (see recipes, page 48).

freezer meatballs

freezer meatballs

3 beaten eggs
¾ cup milk
3 cups soft bread crumbs
½ cup finely chopped onion
3 pounds ground beef

Combine eggs and milk; stir in bread crumbs, onion, and 2 teaspoons *salt*. Add ground beef; mix well. Shape into 1-inch meatballs. Bake meatballs, *half* at a time, in large, shallow baking pan in 375° oven for 25 to 30 minutes. Remove from pan; cool. Arrange cooled meatballs in single layer on baking sheet so edges do not touch. Freeze till firm. Using 24 meatballs per package, wrap meatballs in moisture-vaporproof freezer bags. Seal, label, and freeze. Makes 72.
Note: If desired, substitute *Basic Oven Meatballs* for 24 Freezer Meatballs in recipes on this page and next. *For Basic Oven Meatballs*, in bowl combine 1 beaten *egg* and ¼ cup *milk*. Stir in 1 cup *soft bread crumbs*, 2 tablespoons *chopped onion*, and ¾ teaspoon *salt*. Add 1 pound *ground beef*; mix well. Shape and bake as above. Makes 24. Use hot meatballs as directed for Freezer Meatballs *except* omit thawing directions.

wine-sauced meatballs

Pictured on pages 46 and 47

Assembling time: 10 minutes
Cooking time: 30 minutes

1 large onion, sliced and separated into rings
3 tablespoons butter *or* margarine
3 tablespoons all-purpose flour
1½ cups water
1 tablespoon instant beef bouillon granules
2 teaspoons Worcestershire sauce
½ teaspoon dried thyme, crushed
24 Freezer Meatballs
⅓ cup dry red wine
1 4-ounce can mushroom stems and pieces, drained
Hot cooked noodles
Snipped parsley
Watercress leaves

In 10-inch skillet cook onion in butter or margarine till tender. Blend flour into the onion-butter mixture. Add water, bouillon granules, Worcestershire sauce, and thyme. Cook and stir till thickened and bubbly. Add meatballs, wine, and mushrooms. Cover and simmer for 20 minutes or till meatballs are heated through. Serve over hot cooked noodles. Garnish with snipped parsley and watercress. Makes 6 servings.

meatball-vegetable soup

Assembling time: 5 minutes
Cooking time: 30 minutes

24 Freezer Meatballs
¼ cup water
1 16-ounce can tomatoes, cut up
1 16-ounce can lima beans
2 medium carrots, chopped
1 stalk celery, chopped
1 cup water
2 teaspoons instant beef bouillon granules
½ teaspoon dried thyme, crushed
⅛ teaspoon pepper

To thaw Freezer Meatballs, in large saucepan combine meatballs and ¼ cup water. Cover and simmer for 15 minutes. Break meatballs apart with fork.
  To meatballs, add *undrained* tomatoes, *undrained* lima beans, carrots, celery, 1 cup water, bouillon granules, thyme, and pepper. Bring to boiling. Reduce heat. Cover and simmer for 10 minutes or till meatballs are heated through. Makes 4 to 6 servings.

peppery meatball sandwiches

Pictured on page 53

Total time: 40 minutes

- 24 **Freezer Meatballs**
- 1 **cup water**
- 1 **8-ounce can tomato sauce**
- 1 **6-ounce can tomato paste**
- 2 **teaspoons sugar**
- ½ **teaspoon garlic powder**
- ¼ **teaspoon salt**
- ¼ **teaspoon fennel seed**
- ¼ **teaspoon dried oregano, crushed**
- 8 **French-style rolls**
    Parmesan cheese *or* crushed red pepper (optional)
    Hot peppers

To thaw Freezer Meatballs, in large saucepan combine meatballs and 1 cup water. Bring to boiling. Reduce heat. Cover and simmer for 15 minutes.

To meatballs add tomato sauce, tomato paste, sugar, garlic powder, salt, fennel seed, and oregano. Cover and simmer 15 minutes, stirring occasionally. Meanwhile, halve rolls; hollow out. Fill each roll with 3 meatballs and some sauce. Sprinkle cheese or crushed red pepper over meatballs, if desired. Serve with hot peppers. Makes 8 servings.

creamy meatball casserole

Total time: 45 minutes

- 24 **Freezer Meatballs**
- ¼ **cup water**
- 1 **10¾-ounce can condensed cream of mushroom soup**
- 1 **cup milk**
- 1 **2½-ounce envelope sour cream sauce mix**
- ⅛ **teaspoon pepper**
- 1 **16-ounce can sliced potatoes, drained**
- 1 **8-ounce can diced carrots, drained**
- ¼ **cup fine dry bread crumbs**
- 1 **teaspoon dried parsley flakes**
- 1 **tablespoon butter *or* margarine, melted**

To thaw Freezer Meatballs, in large saucepan combine meatballs and water. Cover and simmer 15 minutes; drain off any liquid.

In a 2-quart casserole combine soup, milk, dry sour cream sauce mix, and pepper. Stir in meatballs, potatoes, and carrots. Stir together bread crumbs, parsley flakes, and melted butter or margarine; sprinkle atop casserole. Bake in a 350° oven about 25 minutes or till heated through. Serves 6.

Microwave directions
In 2-quart nonmetal casserole combine frozen meatballs and water. Cook, covered, in a counter-top microwave oven on high power for 3 to 4 minutes; drain off any liquid. Stir in soup, milk, sour cream sauce mix, pepper, potatoes, and carrots. Top with bread crumb mixture as above. Micro-cook, uncovered, 10 minutes or till heated through, turning dish twice.

sauerbraten meatballs

Total time: 30 minutes

- 1 **13¾-ounce can beef broth**
- ¼ **cup dry red wine**
- 1 **tablespoon vinegar**
- ⅛ **teaspoon ground allspice**
   Dash ground cloves
- 24 **Freezer Meatballs**
- 1 **stalk celery, chopped**
- 8 **gingersnaps, crumbled**
   Cooked shredded cabbage

In 3-quart saucepan combine beef broth, wine, vinegar, allspice, cloves, and ¼ teaspoon *pepper*. Bring to boiling. Add meatballs and celery. Reduce heat. Simmer, covered, for 20 minutes or till meatballs are heated through. Add gingersnaps. Cook and stir till thickened and bubbly. Serve over cooked shredded cabbage. Serves 6.

49

freezer stew mix

START WITH . . .

freezer stew mix

**4 pounds beef round steak,
  cut ¾ inch thick**
2 tablespoons cooking oil
1 cup chopped onion
1 cup chopped celery
¼ cup snipped parsley
**2 tablespoons instant beef
  bouillon granules**
**2 tablespoons
  Worcestershire sauce**

Cut meat into ¾-inch cubes.
In skillet brown the meat in
hot oil. Add remaining ingredients and 1 cup *water*. Bring to
boiling. Cover; simmer 45 to
50 minutes, stirring occasionally. Cool. Spoon the meat-
broth mixture into 4 moisture-
vaporproof containers. Seal,
label, and freeze. Makes about
8 cups.
Note: If desired, substitute
Basic Stew Mix for 2 cups
Freezer Stew Mix in the recipes on this page and next. For
Basic Stew Mix, cook Freezer
Stew Mix as above *except* use
1 pound beef round steak, *1
tablespoon* cooking oil, *¼ cup*
each chopped onion and
celery, *¼ cup* water, *1 tablespoon* snipped parsley, *1½
teaspoons* instant beef bouillon granules, and *1½ teaspoons* Worcestershire sauce.
Makes 2 cups. Use hot as
directed for Freezer Stew
Mix *except* omit thawing
directions.

meat-cabbage skillet

Assembling time: 10 minutes
Cooking time: 35 minutes

2 cups Freezer Stew Mix
**1 small head cabbage
  (1 pound), shredded**
**1 large carrot, thinly sliced
  (½ cup)**
1 medium onion, chopped
**2 teaspoons instant beef
  bouillon granules**
½ teaspoon caraway seed
⅛ teaspoon pepper
1 12-ounce can beer
2 tablespoons cold water
1 tablespoon cornstarch

In a 10-inch skillet place the
Freezer Stew Mix; top with the
cabbage, carrot, onion, bouillon
granules, caraway seed, and
pepper. Pour beer over all.
Cover and cook over medium-
low heat for 15 minutes. Break
up mix with fork. Cover and
continue cooking about 15
minutes more or till vegetables
are tender. Combine cold
water and cornstarch; add to
mixture. Cook and stir till
thickened and bubbly. Cook 1
to 2 minutes more. Makes 4 to
6 servings.

beef burgundy

Total time: 45 minutes

2 cups Freezer Stew Mix
¼ cup water
¾ cup water
½ cup burgundy
**1 1¾-ounce envelope
  mushroom gravy mix**
2 large carrots, sliced
**1 4-ounce can whole
  mushrooms**
2 tablespoons cold water
**1 tablespoon all-purpose
  flour**
Hot cooked noodles
**Snipped parsley
  (optional)**

To thaw Freezer Stew Mix, in
large saucepan combine mix
and ¼ cup water. Cover and
simmer over low heat for 15
minutes; break up mix using a
fork. Cook 5 minutes more.
  Add ¾ cup water, burgundy,
gravy mix, carrots, and *undrained* mushrooms. Bring to
boiling; reduce heat. Cover
and simmer for 15 minutes or
till carrots are tender. Combine
2 tablespoons cold water and
flour; stir into beef mixture.
Cook and stir till thickened and
bubbly; cook 1 to 2 minutes
more. Serve atop noodles.
Sprinkle parsley atop, if desired. Makes 4 servings.

choose-a-vegetable stew

Total time: 1 hour

2 cups Freezer Stew Mix
¼ cup water
1¼ cups water
2 teaspoons instant beef bouillon granules
2 teaspoons horseradish mustard
½ teaspoon dried marjoram, crushed
1 bay leaf
Dash pepper
5 cups fresh *or* frozen vegetables (use any combination of cut-up potatoes, carrots, rutabagas, onion, and celery, *or* green beans, corn, and peas)
1 tablespoon cornstarch

To thaw Freezer Stew Mix, in 3-quart saucepan combine frozen mix and ¼ cup water. Cover and cook over low heat for 15 minutes; break up mix using fork. Cook 5 minutes more.

Combine the 1¼ cups water, bouillon granules, mustard, marjoram, bay leaf, and pepper. Add to meat mixture; bring to boiling. Reduce heat. Add desired vegetables. Cover and simmer 20 to 30 minutes or till vegetables are done. Combine cornstarch and 2 tablespoons *cold water*; add to stew. Cook and stir till thickened and bubbly. Cook 2 minutes more. Serves 4 to 6.

beef and barley soup

Total time: 30 minutes

2 cups Freezer Stew Mix
2¼ cups water
1 16-ounce can tomatoes, cut up
1 4-ounce can mushroom stems and pieces
¾ cup quick-cooking barley
1 tablespoon minced dried onion
1 tablespoon instant beef bouillon granules
½ teaspoon dried thyme, crushed
⅛ teaspoon pepper

In large saucepan place Freezer Stew Mix. Add water, *undrained* tomatoes, *undrained* mushrooms, barley, onion, beef bouillon granules, thyme, and pepper. Bring to boiling. Reduce heat; cover and simmer 20 minutes or till barley is tender. Stir occasionally to separate meat cubes. Turn into serving bowl. Makes 6 servings.

french onion and beef casserole

Total time: 35 minutes

2 cups Freezer Stew Mix
¼ cup water
4 large onions, sliced and separated into rings
1 clove garlic, minced
3 tablespoons butter
1 tablespoon all-purpose flour
⅛ teaspoon pepper
1 10¼-ounce can beef gravy
2 tablespoons dry sherry
6 slices French bread, toasted
1 cup shredded Swiss cheese

To thaw Freezer Stew Mix, in saucepan combine frozen mix and water. Cover; simmer over low heat 15 minutes; break up mix using a fork. Cook 5 minutes more.

Meanwhile, in medium saucepan cook onions and garlic, covered, in butter for 8 to 10 minutes or till tender. Blend in flour and pepper. Add gravy. Cook and stir till bubbly. Add meat mixture. Stir in sherry. Cook and stir 2 minutes more. Place one slice toast in each of 6 au gratin dishes. Top with meat mixture. Sprinkle cheese atop each. Place under broiler for 2 minutes or till cheese is melted. Serves 6.

freezer ground meat mix

freezer ground meat mix

3 beaten eggs
2 cups soft bread crumbs (about 3 slices)
1 cup chopped celery
1 cup chopped onion
1 cup shredded carrot
1 teaspoon salt
3 pounds ground beef *or* ground pork

Combine eggs, bread crumbs, celery, onion, carrot, and salt. Add meat; mix well. In large skillet cook the mixture, *half* at a time, till meat is lightly browned. Stir to break up large pieces of meat. Drain off fat, if necessary. Cool quickly. Spoon 2 cups of meat mixture into each of 5 moisture-vaporproof containers or freezer bags. Seal, label, and freeze. Makes five 2-cup portions.

Note: If desired, substitute *Basic Ground Meat Mix* for 2 cups Freezer Ground Meat Mix in recipes on this and next 3 pages. For Basic Ground Meat Mix, cook 1 pound *ground beef* and ⅓ cup *chopped onion* till meat is browned; drain off fat. Stir in ¼ teaspoon *salt* and ⅛ teaspoon *pepper*. Use hot mixture as directed for Freezer Ground Meat Mix *except* omit thawing directions.

meat and crescent squares

Total time: 45 minutes

2 cups Freezer Ground Meat Mix
1 package (8) refrigerated crescent rolls
1 8-ounce can tomato sauce
1 teaspoon minced dried onion
¼ cup sliced pimiento-stuffed olives
1 2-ounce can sliced mushrooms, drained
¼ teaspoon dried thyme, crushed
4 slices American cheese

To thaw Freezer Ground Meat Mix, in saucepan combine mix and ¼ cup *water*. Cover; cook for 15 minutes; break up with fork. Cook 5 minutes more.

Meanwhile, separate crescent dough into 4 rectangles; press perforations to seal. Press 3 rectangles onto bottom and 1 inch up sides of a 12x7½x2-inch baking dish. Bake in 375° oven 7 minutes.

Combine tomato sauce and onion. Stir in olives, mushrooms, thyme, and ⅛ teaspoon *pepper*. Add meat. Spread mixture atop crust. Cut remaining dough into four triangles; arrange atop casserole. Brush with milk. Bake, uncovered, in 375° oven 20 minutes. Halve cheese slices; arrange atop casserole. Bake 5 minutes. Serves 6.

beef chowder

Total time: 25 minutes

1 17-ounce can cream-style corn
1 16-ounce can tomatoes, cut up
½ cup water
2 tablespoons snipped parsley
1 teaspoon instant beef bouillon granules
¾ teaspoon Worcestershire sauce
¼ teaspoon dried thyme, crushed
⅛ teaspoon pepper
2 cups Freezer Ground Meat Mix

In large saucepan stir together cream-style corn, *undrained* tomatoes, water, snipped parsley, beef bouillon granules, Worcestershire sauce, thyme, and pepper. Add Freezer Ground Meat Mix. Cover and cook over medium heat about 20 minutes or till heated through, stirring frequently. Makes 4 servings.

Meat and Crescent Squares and *Peppery Meatball Sandwiches* (see recipe, page 49) start with make-ahead meat mixtures.

freezer ground meat mix

biscuit meat pie

Assembling time: 30 minutes
Cooking time: 15 minutes

**2 cups Freezer Ground
  Meat Mix**
**1 10-ounce package frozen
  mixed vegetables**
**1 10¾-ounce can
  condensed cream of
  mushroom soup**
1 cup milk
**½ teaspoon dried basil,
  crushed**
1 cup packaged biscuit mix
**¼ cup shredded American
  cheese (2 ounces)**

To thaw Freezer Ground Meat Mix, in large saucepan combine mix and ¼ cup *water*. Cover and cook over low heat for 20 minutes, stirring occasionally. Meanwhile, run hot water over vegetables in colander till partially thawed. To meat mixture add vegetables, soup, milk, basil, and ¼ teaspoon *pepper*. Bring to boiling. Reduce heat; simmer 2 minutes. Meanwhile, combine biscuit mix, cheese, and ¼ cup *water*. Stir till combined. Turn out onto surface dusted with additional biscuit mix; knead 5 or 6 times. Pat or roll out dough to a 7-inch circle. Cut into 6 wedges. Turn *hot* meat mixture into a 2-quart casserole. Immediately top with biscuit wedges. Bake, uncovered, in a 425° oven about 15 minutes or till biscuits are done. Makes 6 servings.

creamy beef and potato casserole

Assembling time: 25 minutes
Cooking time: 40 minutes

**2 cups Freezer Ground
  Meat Mix**
¼ cup water
**1 5½-ounce package dry au
  gratin potatoes**
2 cups milk
¾ cup boiling water
**1 4-ounce can sliced
  mushrooms, drained**
**¼ teaspoon dried thyme,
  crushed**
**¼ cup shredded cheddar
  cheese (1 ounce)**

To thaw Freezer Ground Meat Mix, in saucepan combine mix and ¼ cup water. Cover and cook over low heat for 15 minutes; break up mix using a fork. Cover and cook 5 minutes more. Drain off any liquid.

Meanwhile, in a 2-quart casserole combine dry potatoes, the sauce mix from the potato package, milk, ¾ cup boiling water, mushrooms, and thyme. Stir in the meat mix. Bake in a 400° oven for 30 to 35 minutes. Sprinkle cheese atop edge of casserole. Let stand 5 minutes before serving. Makes 4 to 6 servings.

herbed beef strata

Assembling time: 25 minutes
Cooking time: 45 minutes

**2 cups Freezer Ground
  Meat Mix**
**1 7-ounce package herb-
  seasoned stuffing
  croutons (5 cups)**
4 eggs
1½ cups milk
**1 11-ounce can
  condensed cheddar
  cheese soup**
**½ cup mayonnaise *or*
  salad dressing**
**2 teaspoons minced dried
  onion**
⅛ teaspoon pepper
**1 tablespoon butter,
  melted**

To thaw Freezer Ground Meat Mix, in saucepan combine mix and ¼ cup *water*. Cover; cook over low heat 15 minutes; break up mix using a fork. Cover; cook 5 minutes more.

Place *2 cups* of the croutons in an 8x8x2-inch baking dish. Top with meat mixture. Place *2 cups* croutons atop meat. Beat together eggs, milk, soup, mayonnaise, onion, and pepper. Pour evenly over croutons. Toss remaining 1 cup croutons with the butter; sprinkle atop baking dish. Bake, uncovered, in 325° oven about 40 minutes or till knife inserted off center comes out clean. Let stand 5 minutes before serving. Serves 6.

54

stir-fried beef and vegetables

Assembling time: 20 minutes
Cooking time: 8 minutes

- **2 cups Freezer Ground Meat Mix**
- **1 6-ounce package frozen pea pods**
- **1 teaspoon instant beef bouillon granules**
- **⅓ cup soy sauce**
- **4 teaspoons cornstarch**
- **1 teaspoon sugar**
- **2 tablespoons cooking oil**
- **1 medium onion, sliced and separated into rings**
- **2 stalks celery, bias sliced (1 cup)**
- **1 8-ounce can sliced water chestnuts, drained**
- **Hot cooked rice**

To thaw Freezer Ground Meat Mix, in saucepan combine mix and ¼ cup *water*. Cover and cook over low heat for 15 minutes; break up mix using a fork. Cover; cook 5 minutes more.

Meanwhile, run hot water over pea pods in colander till partially thawed. In small bowl dissolve bouillon granules in 1 cup *boiling water*; stir in soy sauce. Combine cornstarch and sugar; stir into the soy mixture. Set aside.

Preheat a wok or large skillet over high heat; add oil. Stir-fry onion and celery in hot oil for 2 minutes. Add water chestnuts and meat mixture; stir-fry 1 minute more. Push mixture from center of wok or skillet. Stir bouillon mixture; add to center of wok or skillet. Cook and stir till thickened and bubbly. Add pea pods to wok; stir all together. Cover; cook 1 minute. Serve with rice. Makes 4 servings.

saucepan spaghetti sauce

Total time: 40 minutes

- **2 cups Freezer Ground Meat Mix**
- **1 15-ounce can tomato sauce**
- **1 teaspoon dried oregano, crushed**
- **1 teaspoon Worcestershire sauce**
- **½ teaspoon sugar**
- **½ teaspoon dried basil, crushed**
- **¼ teaspoon garlic powder**
- **Hot cooked spaghetti**
- **Grated Parmesan cheese**

To thaw Freezer Ground Meat Mix, in saucepan combine mix and ¼ cup *water*. Cover; cook over low heat 15 minutes. Break up mix using fork.

To meat mixture, add tomato sauce, oregano, Worcestershire sauce, sugar, basil, garlic powder, ¼ teaspoon *salt*, and ⅛ teaspoon *pepper*. Bring to boiling; reduce heat. Simmer, uncovered, about 15 minutes, stirring occasionally. Serve over spaghetti. Pass cheese. Serves 4.

chow mein

Total time: 35 minutes

- **2 cups Freezer Ground Meat Mix**
- **1 10-ounce package frozen Japanese-style vegetables**
- **¼ cup sliced green onion**
- **¼ teaspoon ground ginger**
- **3 tablespoons soy sauce**
- **2 tablespoons cold water**
- **1 tablespoon cornstarch**
- **1 3-ounce can chow mein noodles**

To thaw Freezer Ground Meat Mix, in saucepan combine mix and ⅔ cup *water*. Cover and cook over low heat for 15 minutes; break up mix using a fork.

To meat mixture add frozen vegetables; cook 5 minutes. Add green onion and ginger. Combine soy sauce, the 2 tablespoons cold water and the cornstarch; stir into beef mixture. Cook and stir till thickened and bubbly. Cook and stir 1 to 2 minutes more. Serve over chow mein noodles. Makes 4 servings.

55

cooked meat

START WITH...

roasted pork, beef, or lamb

1 4- to 6-pound pork shoulder blade Boston roast *or* boneless beef round rump roast, *or* one 3- to 5-pound boneless lamb shoulder

Before roasting pork, beef, or lamb, trim off excess fat. Season meat with salt and pepper. Place meat, fat side up, on a rack in a shallow roasting pan.

Insert a meat thermometer so its bulb rests in the center of the thickest portion of the meat and does not rest in fat or touch bone. Do not add any liquids and do not cover roasting pan.

Roast meat in a 325° oven till meat thermometer registers desired internal temperature.

For easier carving, let the meat stand about 15 minutes.

Use the roasting times and temperatures given in the chart below as guides to the total cooking time for the cut of meat you are preparing. **Note:** Cook these common roasts to cut up and freeze for later use in the following recipes. Or, use leftover beef, pork, or lamb.

freezing cooked meat

Rapidly cool cooked meat before freezing. Place cooked meat on a rack to cool. Or, place into bowl; immerse bowl in cold water.

Chop or slice meat as directed in the recipes you plan to use. Freeze 1- to 2-cup portions in moisture-vaporproof containers. Seal, label, and freeze.

Cooked meat can be stored in the freezer for 2 to 3 months. Thaw frozen meat in refrigerator or defrost in a microwave oven.

Note: One pound boneless cooked meat is approximately 3 cups chopped *or* 2 cups cubed.

skip-a-step stroganoff

Total time: 30 minutes

- **1 6-ounce can sliced mushrooms**
- **1 medium onion, sliced**
- **⅓ cup dry sherry *or* dry white wine**
- **¼ cup water**
- **½ teaspoon instant beef bouillon granules**
- **2 cups cooked beef cut into bite-size strips**
- **1 cup dairy sour cream**
- **2 tablespoons all-purpose flour**
- **Hot cooked noodles**

In saucepan combine *un-drained* mushrooms and the onion slices; cook, covered, over low heat for 5 minutes. Add sherry or wine, water, and bouillon granules; stir in meat. Cover; cook for 5 minutes. Combine sour cream and flour; stir a small amount of the hot mixture into the sour cream; return all to saucepan. Cook and stir till thickened and bubbly. Cook and stir 1 to 2 minutes more. Serve over hot cooked noodles. Makes 4 servings.

meat	internal temperature	approximate cooking time
BEEF	150° to 170°	2 to 2½ hrs.
PORK	170°	3 to 4 hrs.
LAMB	160° (medium)	2 to 3 hrs.

Nice ✓

quick batch chili

Assembling time: 20 minutes
Cooking time: 25 minutes

1 16-ounce can tomatoes, cut up
2 cups chopped cooked beef *or* pork
1 15½-ounce can red kidney beans
½ of a 6-ounce can (⅓ cup) tomato paste
¼ cup water
3 tablespoons diced dried bell pepper
1½ teaspoons minced dried onion
1½ teaspoons chili powder
½ teaspoon dried oregano, crushed
¼ teaspoon salt
¼ teaspoon ground cumin
Dash garlic powder

In a 4-quart Dutch oven or kettle combine *undrained* tomatoes, beef or pork, the *undrained* kidney beans, the tomato paste, water, dried bell pepper, dried onion, chili powder, oregano, salt, cumin, and garlic powder. Bring to boiling; simmer, covered, for 20 minutes. Makes 4 servings.

creamy beef with poppy seed

Total time: 40 minutes

1 single-serving envelope instant onion soup mix
1 teaspoon dried parsley flakes
½ cup hot water
1 cup cream-style cottage cheese
¾ cup dairy sour cream
3 cups chopped cooked beef *or* pork
½ cup sliced pitted ripe olives *mushrooms oregon*
1 teaspoon poppy seed
Hot cooked noodles

Stir onion soup mix and dried parsley flakes into the hot water; set aside. In blender container combine cottage cheese and sour cream. Cover and blend till smooth. In large saucepan combine soup mixture, cottage cheese mixture, cooked meat, *half* of the olives, and the poppy seed; heat through. Serve over hot cooked noodles. Garnish with remaining olives. Makes 6 servings.

barbecue-sauced pork sandwiches

Total time: 20 minutes

1 8-ounce can tomato sauce with mushrooms
2 tablespoons vinegar
1 tablespoon diced dried bell pepper
1 tablespoon Worcestershire sauce
2 teaspoons brown sugar
1 teaspoon minced dried onion
Few dashes bottled hot pepper sauce
2 cups cooked pork cut into bite-size strips
4 French-style rolls

In large saucepan combine tomato sauce, vinegar, dried bell pepper, Worcestershire sauce, brown sugar, dried onion, and hot pepper sauce. Bring to boiling; reduce heat and simmer, uncovered, about 3 minutes. Stir in pork; cover and cook about 2 minutes more or till heated through. Meanwhile, split and toast rolls. Spoon pork mixture onto bottom half of each roll; top with other roll half. Makes 4 servings.

cooked meat

lamb chowder with dumplings

Total time: 40 minutes

- **1 stalk celery, chopped**
- **2 tablespoons butter**
- **3 tablespoons all-purpose flour**
- **1 tablespoon minced dried onion**
- **1½ teaspoons prepared mustard (optional)**
- **½ teaspoon dried marjoram, crushed**
- **1 13¾-ounce can chicken broth**
- **1 cup milk**
- **¾ cup shredded American cheese (3 ounces)**
- **1 10-ounce package frozen cut broccoli**
- **1½ cups chopped cooked lamb**
- **1 cup packaged biscuit mix**
- **1 teaspoon dried parsley flakes**
- **⅓ cup milk**

Cook celery in butter till tender. Stir in flour, onion, mustard, marjoram, and ½ teaspoon *salt*. Add broth and the 1 cup milk. Cook and stir till thickened and bubbly. Cook and stir 1 to 2 minutes more. Stir in cheese till melted. Meanwhile, run hot water over broccoli in a colander till partially thawed. Add broccoli and lamb to sauce; bring to boiling.

Use refrigerated crescent roll dough to make the easy, golden crust for *Quick Crescent Quiche.*

Meanwhile, combine biscuit mix and parsley; stir in the ⅓ cup milk. Drop from a tablespoon to make 8 dumplings atop bubbling soup. Simmer, uncovered, for 10 minutes. Cover; simmer 10 minutes more. Serves 4.

macaroni pork salad

Total time: 20 minutes

- **4 ounces corkscrew macaroni (1⅔ cups)**
- **1 cup dairy sour cream**
- **½ cup Caesar salad dressing**
- **2 tablespoons milk**
- **8 ounces cheddar cheese, cubed (2 cups)**
- **1 cup chopped cooked pork**
- **¼ cup chopped green pepper**
- **8 tomato slices**
  Lettuce

Cook macaroni according to package directions. Rinse with cold water; drain. Meanwhile, combine sour cream, salad dressing, and milk. In bowl combine cheese, pork, green pepper, and macaroni. Add sour cream mixture; toss lightly. Chill till serving time or serve immediately. To serve, place 2 tomato slices on each of 4 lettuce-lined plates; top with macaroni. Serves 4.
Note: Substitute elbow macaroni for the corkscrew macaroni, if desired.

quick crescent quiche

Assembling time: 15 minutes
Cooking time: 30 minutes

- **1 package (8) refrigerated crescent rolls**
- **1 cup chopped cooked pork, lamb,. *or* beef**
- **1 4-ounce can sliced mushrooms, drained**
- **1 cup shredded Swiss cheese (4 ounces)**
- **2 beaten eggs**
- **1 5⅓-ounce can (⅔ cup) evaporated milk**
- **2 teaspoons diced bell pepper**
- **¼ teaspoon dried thyme, crushed**
- **Few dashes bottled hot pepper sauce**
- **¼ cup slivered almonds**
- **1 tablespoon snipped parsley**

Separate rolls into 8 triangles. In ungreased 9-inch pie plate or quiche dish place dough triangles with points toward center; press over bottom and up sides. Sprinkle pork, lamb, or beef and mushrooms onto bottom. Top with Swiss cheese.

Combine eggs, evaporated milk, dried pepper, thyme, and hot pepper sauce. Pour over cheese. Sprinkle almonds and parsley atop. Cover crust edges using foil to prevent overbrowning. Bake in 350° oven about 30 minutes or till almost set. Serves 6.

59

cooked poultry

roasted chicken or turkey

1 4- to 5-pound whole roasting chicken *or* one 8- to 12-pound turkey

Rinse bird and pat dry with paper toweling. Rub inside cavity with salt. Skewer neck skin to back. Tie legs to tail; twist wing tips under back.

Place bird, breast side up, on a rack in a shallow roasting pan. Brush skin of bird using cooking oil. Insert meat thermometer into center of inside thigh muscle, making sure bulb does not touch bone. Cover bird loosely with foil. (For turkey, press foil lightly at the end of drumsticks and neck; leave air space between bird and foil.) Roast in uncovered pan, according to the chart below. Baste bird occasionally with pan drippings. When bird is two-thirds done, cut string between legs so thighs will cook evenly. (For turkey, remove foil about 45 minutes before bird is done.) Continue roasting till done.

Bird is done when meat thermometer registers 185° and leg moves easily in the socket. Remove bird from oven. Let stand 15 minutes before cutting up.

Note: Roast, chop, and freeze chicken or turkey to have it on hand for last-minute meals.

storing cooked poultry

If cooked poultry is used within two days, store it in the refrigerator. Otherwise, freeze it immediately.

Remove the meat from the bones. Cool. Chop meat and divide it into 2 cup portions. Wrap tightly in moisture-vapor-proof containers; seal, label, and freeze. Use within one month.

Thaw frozen cooked poultry in the refrigerator. For faster thawing, place the poultry in a watertight container and immerse in *cool* water. Do not refreeze cooked poultry after it has been thawed.

poultry	oven temperature	approximate cooking time
CHICKEN	375°	2 to 2½ hours
TURKEY	325°	4 to 4½ hours

chicken tetrazzini

Total time: 20 minutes

½ **cup sliced green onion**
3 **tablespoons butter *or* margarine**
¼ **cup all-purpose flour**
¼ **teaspoon salt**
¼ **teaspoon pepper**
1 **13¾-ounce can chicken broth**
1 **5¾-ounce can evaporated milk**
2 **cups chopped cooked chicken *or* turkey**
1 **6-ounce can sliced mushrooms, drained**
¼ **cup dry white wine**
½ **cup grated Parmesan cheese**
Hot cooked spaghetti

In large saucepan cook onion in butter or margarine till tender. Stir in flour, salt, and pepper. Add chicken broth and evaporated milk. Cook and stir till thickened and bubbly. Cook 2 minutes more. Stir in chicken or turkey, mushrooms, and wine. Heat through. On large serving platter spoon sauce over hot cooked spaghetti. Sprinkle cheese atop. Toss lightly. Makes 6 servings.

turkey-broccoli casseroles

Assembling time: 20 minutes
Cooking time: 30 minutes

- **3 ounces medium noodles**
- **1 10-ounce package frozen cut broccoli**
- **1 10¾-ounce can condensed cream of onion soup**
- **1 cup dairy sour cream**
- **½ cup milk**
- **2 cups chopped cooked turkey *or* chicken**
- **1 8-ounce can sliced water chestnuts, drained**
- **½ cup shredded Swiss cheese**
- **Paprika**

Cook noodles according to package directions; drain. Cook broccoli according to package directions; drain. Combine condensed soup, sour cream, and milk. Stir in turkey or chicken, water chestnuts, cheese, noodles, and broccoli. Season. Divide mixture evenly into six 10-ounce casseroles. Sprinkle with paprika. Bake in a 350° oven 25 to 30 minutes. Serves 6.

Microwave directions

Cook noodles and broccoli as above. Combine all ingredients as above *except* paprika. Turn mixture into six 10-ounce nonmetal casseroles. Micro-cook, uncovered, in a counter-top microwave oven on high power about 8 minutes, turning casseroles after 4 minutes.

mexican turkey bake

Assembling time: 20 minutes
Cooking time: 25 minutes

- **1 10¾-ounce can condensed cream of onion soup**
- **¾ cup chicken broth**
- **2 cups chopped cooked turkey *or* chicken**
- **1 12-ounce can whole kernel corn with sweet peppers *or* whole kernel corn, drained**
- **2 cups shredded Monterey Jack cheese (8 ounces)**
- **6 cornmeal tortillas, each cut into 8 wedges**
- **1 4-ounce can green chili peppers, rinsed, seeded, and chopped**
- **¼ cup sliced pitted ripe olives**

In bowl combine condensed soup and chicken broth. Stir in chicken or turkey, corn, *1½ cups* of the cheese, the tortillas, chili peppers, and olives. Turn mixture into an ungreased 8x8x2-inch baking dish; sprinkle remaining cheese atop. Bake, uncovered, in a 400° oven about 25 minutes or till heated through. Makes 6 servings.

spicy turkey skillet

Total time: 30 minutes

- **1 medium green pepper, cut into strips**
- **1 medium onion, cut into wedges**
- **1 clove garlic, minced**
- **2 tablespoons butter *or* margarine**
- **1½ cups quick-cooking rice**
- **1 16-ounce can tomatoes, cut up**
- **½ of a 1½-ounce envelope (2 tablespoons) chili seasoning mix**
- **1 teaspoon sugar**
- **1 teaspoon instant chicken bouillon granules**
- **¼ cup cold water**
- **1 teaspoon cornstarch**
- **2 cups chopped cooked turkey *or* chicken**

In 10-inch skillet cook green pepper, onion, and garlic in butter or margarine till tender. Meanwhile, prepare rice according to package directions. To vegetables in skillet, add *undrained* tomatoes, chili seasoning mix, sugar, and bouillon granules. Combine cold water and cornstarch; add to vegetable mixture. Cook and stir till thickened and bubbly. Add turkey or chicken. Cook, covered, 3 to 4 minutes or till heated through. Serve over rice. Makes 4 servings.

61

cooked poultry

cantonese turkey

Assembling time: 20 minutes
Cooking time: 15 minutes

2 stalks celery, bias sliced
2 medium carrots, thinly
**   sliced**
1 medium onion, chopped
3 tablespoons butter *or*
**   margarine**
1 15¼-ounce can pineapple
**   chunks (juice pack)**
1 cup water
1 teaspoon instant chicken
**   bouillon granules**
¼ cup soy sauce
2 tablespoons cornstarch
2 cups chopped cooked
**   turkey**
**   Hot cooked rice**
¼ cup sliced almonds

In large saucepan cook celery, carrots, and onion in butter or margarine, covered, about 5 minutes or till tender. Add *undrained* pineapple, water, and bouillon granules; bring to boiling. Combine soy sauce and cornstarch; stir into vegetable mixture. Cook and stir till thickened and bubbly. Cook and stir 1 to 2 minutes more. Stir in turkey; heat through. Serve over hot cooked rice. Sprinkle almonds atop. Makes 5 servings.

Combine cooked turkey with pineapple, celery, and carrot for a speedy version of *Cantonese Turkey.*

biscuit-topped chicken pies

Pictured on pages 46 and 47

Total time: 30 minutes

3 tablespoons cornstarch
1 tablespoon minced dried
**   onion**
½ teaspoon poultry
**   seasoning**
⅛ teaspoon pepper
1 10¾-ounce can
**   condensed chicken**
**   broth**
1 cup light cream *or* milk
2 cups chopped cooked
**   chicken**
1 10-ounce package frozen
**   mixed vegetables**
1 3-ounce package cream
**   cheese, cubed**
1 package (6) refrigerated
**   biscuits**
**   Sesame seed**

Stir cornstarch, dried onion, poultry seasoning, and pepper into chicken broth and cream or milk. Cook and stir till thickened and bubbly. Add chicken and frozen vegetables. Heat till bubbly; cook 1 minute more. Stir in cream cheese till melted. Turn mixture into six 10-ounce casseroles. Quarter the biscuits; place 4 pieces atop *hot* filling in each casserole. Sprinkle with sesame seed. Bake in a 450° oven for 8 to 10 minutes. Garnish with cherry tomatoes and curly endive, if desired. Serves 6.

chicken asparagus casserole

Assembling time: 25 minutes
Cooking time: 18 minutes

1 10-ounce package frozen
**   cut asparagus**
2 tablespoons butter *or*
**   margarine**
2 tablespoons all-purpose
**   flour**
1 cup milk
½ cup dairy sour cream
2 tablespoons grated
**   Parmesan cheese**
2 cups chopped cooked
**   chicken *or* turkey**
¼ cup grated Parmesan
**   cheese**
**   Paprika (optional)**

Cook asparagus according to package directions; drain well. Meanwhile, in saucepan melt butter or margarine; blend in flour. Add milk all at once. Cook and stir till thickened and bubbly. Cook and stir 1 to 2 minutes more. Remove from heat; stir in sour cream. Arrange asparagus in a 10x6x2-inch baking dish. Sprinkle with the 2 tablespoons cheese; top with chicken or turkey. Pour sauce over all. Sprinkle the ¼ cup Parmesan cheese over all. Bake in a 400° oven for 15 to 18 minutes or till lightly browned. If desired, sprinkle paprika atop. Makes 4 servings.

freezer casseroles

beef and rice casseroles

Assembling time: 45 minutes
Cooking time: 50 minutes

- **1 6-ounce package regular long grain and wild rice mix**
- **1½ pounds beef round steak, cut into thin bite-size strips**
- **2 tablespoons cooking oil**
- **1 tablespoon instant beef bouillon granules**
- **1 tablespoon minced dried onion**
- **1 6-ounce can sliced mushrooms, drained**
- **1 2-ounce jar sliced pimiento, drained**
- **2 teaspoons lemon juice**

Prepare rice mix according to package directions, cooking just till tender. Meanwhile, in skillet brown meat, *half* at a time, in hot oil. Return all meat to skillet; add bouillon granules, dried onion, and ⅓ cup *water*. Cover; simmer 20 minutes. Remove from heat. Stir in rice, mushrooms, pimiento, and lemon juice. Divide mixture among six 10-ounce casseroles. Cool. Cover with moisture-vaporproof wrap. Seal, label, and freeze.

Bake frozen casseroles, covered, in 400° oven about 50 minutes, stirring once. (Or, bake unfrozen casseroles, covered, in 350° oven about 15 minutes.) Makes 6 casseroles, 1 serving each.

tostada lasagna

Assembling time: 60 minutes
Cooking time: 1½ hours

- **2 pounds ground beef**
- **1 medium onion, chopped**
- **1 28-ounce can tomatoes, cut up**
- **1 8-ounce can tomato sauce**
- **1 teaspoon dried oregano, crushed**
- **1 teaspoon chili powder**
- **½ teaspoon crushed red pepper**
- **1 15½-ounce can red kidney beans, drained**
- **16 lasagna noodles, cooked**
- **4 cups shredded Monterey Jack cheese**
- **Shredded lettuce**
- **Tortilla chips**
- **Cherry tomatoes, halved**

Cook meat and onion till browned. Drain off fat. Stir in next 5 ingredients and 1½ teaspoons *salt*. Simmer, uncovered, 25 minutes. Stir in beans. Using two 10x6x2-inch baking dishes, arrange 4 noodles in each. Spread ¼ meat mixture and ½ of the cheese atop *each*. Repeat layers. Cover, seal, label, and freeze.

Bake frozen casserole, covered, in a 400° oven 1¼ hours. Uncover; bake 10 minutes. (Or, bake unfrozen casserole, covered, in 350° oven 15 minutes. Uncover; bake 10 minutes.) Top with lettuce, chips, and tomatoes. Makes 2 casseroles, 6 servings each.

sausage-crouton casseroles

Assembling time: 30 minutes
Cooking time: 50 minutes

- **1 12-ounce package fully cooked smoked sausage links, sliced**
- **¼ cup milk**
- **1 teaspoon all-purpose flour**
- **1 11-ounce can condensed cheddar cheese soup**
- **1 cup frozen peas**
- **½ cup elbow macaroni, cooked and drained**
- **1 tablespoon minced dried onion**
- **½ teaspoon dried sage, crushed**
- **4 teaspoons butter**
- **1 cup herb-seasoned croutons**

Combine milk and flour. Add sausage, soup, peas, macaroni, onion, and sage. Turn into four 10-ounce casseroles. Cover, seal, label; freeze.

Bake frozen casserole, uncovered, in 400° oven 45 minutes. Meanwhile, for *each* casserole, melt *1 teaspoon* butter; toss with ¼ *cup* croutons. Sprinkle croutons around casserole edge. Bake in 350° oven 5 minutes more. (Or, top unfrozen casserole with buttered croutons; bake in 350° oven 30 minutes.) Makes 4 casseroles, 1 serving each.

Make *Sausage-Crouton Casseroles* and *Tostada Lasagna* to freeze now, heat and serve later.

64

freezer casseroles

beef chili bake

Assembling time: 30 minutes
Cooking time: 65 minutes

- **1 pound ground beef**
- **2 medium onions, chopped**
- **1 10¾-ounce can condensed tomato soup**
- **1 1¼-ounce envelope chili seasoning mix**
- **2 slightly beaten eggs**
- **1 cup milk**
- **2 cups corn *or* tortilla chips, crushed**
- **1 cup shredded Monterey Jack cheese (4 ounces)**
- **Dairy sour cream**
- **Shredded American cheese**

Cook beef and onions till meat is browned; drain off excess fat. Stir in soup, seasoning mix, and ½ cup *water*; simmer about 5 minutes. Combine eggs and milk; stir into meat mixture all at once. Cook and stir till bubbly. Stir in chips and Monterey Jack cheese. Divide mixture between two 1-quart casseroles. Cover; seal, label, and freeze.

Bake frozen casserole, uncovered, in 350° oven about 1 hour. Spread sour cream (about ¼ cup) around edge of casserole; sprinkle American cheese (about ¼ cup) atop. Bake, uncovered, till cheese melts. (Or, bake unfrozen casserole, uncovered, in 350° oven 30 minutes. Continue as above.) Makes 2 casseroles, 4 servings each.

apricot chop bake

Assembling time: 30 minutes
Cooking time: 1 hour

- **8 pork chops, cut ½ inch thick**
- **3 tablespoons cooking oil**
- **1 tablespoon brown sugar**
- **2 teaspoons cornstarch**
- **½ teaspoon ground allspice**
- **1 cup apricot preserves**
- **¾ cup water**
- **1 tablespoon vinegar**
- **½ of an 8-ounce package (¾ cup) dried apricots**
- **2 12-ounce cans fried rice**
- **½ cup raisins**
- **½ cup chopped green pepper**

Brown chops, 4 at a time, in hot oil. Season. Set chops aside; reserve *2 tablespoons* drippings. Stir brown sugar, cornstarch, and allspice into drippings. Stir in apricot preserves, water, and vinegar; bring to boiling. Cook and stir till thickened and bubbly. Cook and stir 1 to 2 minutes more.

Snip apricots; combine with rice, raisins, and green pepper; divide between two 9x9x2-inch baking pans. Arrange 4 chops atop each casserole; pour sauce over each. Cover; seal, label, and freeze.

Bake frozen casserole, covered, in 400° oven about 1 hour. (Or, bake unfrozen casserole, covered, in 350° oven for 35 to 40 minutes.) Makes 2 casseroles, 4 servings each.

creamy ham and mac casserole

Assembling time: 20 minutes
Cooking time: 45 minutes

- **1 cup elbow macaroni**
- **⅔ cup milk**
- **1 10¾-ounce can condensed cream of celery soup**
- **2 cups cubed fully cooked ham**
- **1 4-ounce package shredded sharp cheddar cheese**
- **1 4-ounce can sliced mushrooms, drained**
- **1 teaspoon diced dried bell pepper**
- **1 cup cornflake crumbs**
- **2 tablespoons butter**

Cook macaroni according to package directions *except* omit salt; drain. In bowl stir milk into soup. Add ham, cheese, mushrooms, and dried pepper. Stir in macaroni; mix well.

Divide mixture between two 1-quart casseroles. Cover; seal, label, and freeze.

Bake frozen casserole, covered, in a 400° oven about 40 minutes. For each casserole melt *half* the butter; toss with *half* the cornflake crumbs. Sprinkle atop casserole; bake, uncovered, 5 minutes more. (Or, bake unfrozen casserole, covered, in 350° oven 35 minutes. Uncover; sprinkle cornflake mixture atop as above; bake 5 minutes more.) Makes 2 casseroles, 4 servings each.

seafood tetrazzini

Assembling time: 25 minutes
Cooking time: 1 hour

¾ pound fresh scallops
1 teaspoon minced dried
** onion**
1 16-ounce package frozen
** peeled and deveined**
** shrimp**
¼ cup butter *or* margarine
¼ cup all-purpose flour
1 teaspoon paprika
1 teaspoon dried dillweed
** Few dashes bottled hot**
** pepper sauce**
1 cup milk
2 slightly beaten eggs
1 cup shredded Swiss
** cheese**
1 6-ounce can sliced
** mushrooms**
8 ounces spaghetti, broken
¼ cup grated Romano
** cheese**

Halve any large scallops. Combine dried onion, 2 cups *water,* and ⅛ teaspoon *pepper*; bring to boiling. Add scallops and shrimp; return to boiling. Cover; simmer 1 minute. Drain, reserving *1 cup* liquid.

Melt butter in saucepan. Stir in flour, paprika, dillweed, and hot pepper sauce. Add reserved cooking liquid and the milk. Cook and stir till thickened. Cook and stir 2 minutes more. Slowly stir *half* the hot mixture into beaten eggs; return to hot mixture in saucepan. Add Swiss cheese; stir to melt. Stir in *undrained* mush-

rooms and seafood. Meanwhile, cook spaghetti according to package directions; drain. Divide spaghetti between two 10x6x2-inch baking dishes. Spoon *half* the seafood-cheese mixture atop each; sprinkle with Romano cheese. Cover; seal, label, and freeze.

Bake frozen casserole, uncovered, in 400° oven 1 hour. (Or, bake unfrozen casserole, uncovered, in 350° oven 25 to 30 minutes.) Makes 2 casseroles, 6 servings each.

mushroom lasagna

Assembling time: 25 minutes
Cooking time: 1½ hours

12 lasagna noodles
2 slightly beaten eggs
3 cups cream-style
** cottage cheese**
1 cup shredded mozzarella
** cheese (4 ounces)**
1 cup shredded provolone
** cheese (4 ounces)**
1 16-ounce can tomatoes,
** cut up**
2 tablespoons all-purpose
** flour**
2 tablespoons minced
** dried onion**
2 tablespoons dried
** parsley flakes**
1 teaspoon dried basil,
** crushed**
4 4-ounce cans sliced
** mushrooms, drained**
1 cup grated Parmesan
** cheese**

Cook noodles in boiling salted water just till tender; drain. Combine eggs, cottage cheese, mozzarella cheese, provolone cheese, 1 teaspoon *salt,* and ¼ teaspoon *pepper*; set aside. Combine *undrained* tomatoes, the flour, onion, parsley, and basil; stir in mushrooms. Grease two 10x6x2-inch baking pans. Arrange 2 noodles in bottom of each pan. Divide ⅓ of the cheese mixture between pans; spread over noodles. Divide ⅓ of the mushroom mixture between pans, spreading over cheese mixture. Sprinkle 2 tablespoons Parmesan cheese atop each. Repeat the layers of noodles, cheese mixture, mushroom mixture, and Parmesan cheese twice. Cover; seal, label, and freeze.

Bake frozen casserole, covered, in 400° oven 1½ hours. (Or, bake unfrozen casserole, covered, in 350° oven 40 to 45 minutes.) Let stand 10 minutes. Makes 2 casseroles, 4 servings each.

SHORTCUT TIP: FREEZING CASSEROLES

To freeze casseroles, quickly cool, then cover with moisture-vaporproof wrap such as freezer paper, foil, or plastic wrap.

For best quality, bake frozen casseroles within 3 months.

fast-and-easy
SIDE DISHES

Side-dish recipes, as you'll find on the following pages, can be flavorful yet easy enhancers to your main dish. Prepare the recipes that meet your needs—from a snap-to-put-together bread to a make-ahead-and-forget salad. Transform frozen and canned vegetables into special side dishes with help from *Quick Vegetable Fix-Ups*. And now you can savor fresh homemade bread even when you are tight on time, using our special short-cut recipes. Partially prepare traditional yeast breads, then store the dough in the refrigerator for 2 to 24 hours. Bake the bread when you have the time.

Pictured: *Romano Sesame Rolls* are a quick and delicious disguise for refrigerated crescent rolls (see recipe, page 77). *Orange Rolls* are a variation of *Refrig-a-Rise Dinner Rolls* topped with an orange glaze (see recipes, page 80). And *Pasta Primavera*, a lively combination of linguine and vegetables, goes together in minutes (see recipe, page 81).

vegetables

cheese-asparagus soup

Total time: 15 minutes

- 1 10½-ounce can condensed beef broth
- 1 10-ounce package frozen cut asparagus
- ½ cup chopped celery
- 1 tablespoon minced dried onion
- 1 cup cream-style cottage cheese
- 1½ cups milk
- ½ teaspoon salt
- ⅛ teaspoon pepper
- 5 slices American cheese (5 ounces)
- ½ cup plain yogurt
  Celery leaves (optional)

In 3-quart saucepan stir together beef broth, frozen asparagus, chopped celery, and dried onion; bring to boiling. Reduce heat; cover and simmer about 8 minutes or till vegetables are tender. Transfer asparagus mixture to blender container; add cottage cheese. Cover and blend till smooth. Return mixture to saucepan. Stir in milk, salt, and pepper. Add American cheese; cook and stir till cheese melts. Top each serving with a dollop of yogurt. Garnish with celery leaves, if desired. Makes 6 servings.

spanish corn skillet

Total time: 15 minutes

- 1 small green pepper, cut into 1-inch strips
- 1 tablespoon butter *or* margarine
- 1 15-ounce can Spanish rice
- 1 12-ounce can whole kernel corn, drained
- 1 teaspoon minced dried onion
- ½ teaspoon Worcestershire sauce
  Few dashes ground red pepper
  Few dashes bottled hot pepper sauce
- ½ of a 4-ounce package (½ cup) shredded sharp cheddar cheese

In saucepan cook green pepper in butter or margarine till tender. Stir in Spanish rice, corn, dried onion, Worcestershire sauce, red pepper, and hot pepper sauce. Heat through. Turn into serving dish; sprinkle with cheese. Makes 6 servings.

broccoli bread bake

Assembling time: 15 minutes
Cooking time: 25 minutes

- 1 10-ounce package frozen broccoli spears
- 1 beaten egg
- 1 10¾-ounce can condensed cream of onion soup
- ¼ cup finely chopped celery
- 1 teaspoon dried parsley flakes
- ¼ teaspoon dried tarragon, crushed
  Dash pepper
- 1 package (6) refrigerated flaky dinner rolls
- ¼ cup milk

Cook broccoli according to package directions just till tender; drain well. Meanwhile, combine egg, *half* of the soup, the celery, parsley, tarragon, and pepper. Separate dinner rolls; snip each into quarters. Stir dinner roll pieces into soup mixture. Arrange broccoli spears crosswise in a 10x6x2-inch baking dish. Spoon soup mixture down center of broccoli. Bake in 350° oven for 20 to 25 minutes or till dinner rolls are golden. Meanwhile, in saucepan combine remaining soup and the milk; heat through and serve over baked casserole. Makes 6 servings.

quick vegetable fix-ups

oniony beans

Prepare one 9-ounce package frozen *green beans* according to package directions; drain. Melt 3 tablespoons *butter;* stir in ½ teaspoon *minced dried onion,* ¼ teaspoon *Worcestershire sauce,* and dash *pepper.* Toss with beans. Serves 4.

herbed vegetables

Prepare one 10-ounce package frozen *mixed vegetables* according to package directions; drain. Stir in 3 tablespoons *butter;* ⅛ teaspoon dried *thyme,* crushed; and ⅛ teaspoon *ground sage.* Heat till butter melts. Serves 4.

italian vegetables

Combine one 8¼-ounce can *whole small carrots,* drained; one 8-ounce can *cut green beans,* drained; and one 4-ounce jar *pickled mushrooms,* drained. Stir in ⅓ cup *Italian salad dressing.* Chill. Serves 6.

baked beans olé

Combine one 16-ounce can *pork and beans in tomato sauce,* ½ cup shredded *sharp cheddar cheese,* and 1 teaspoon *chili powder.* Heat through. Serves 4.

beans with dressing

Prepare one 9-ounce package frozen *French-style green beans or* one 10-ounce package frozen *asparagus spears* according to package directions; drain. Stir in ½ teaspoon *salad seasoning.* Serve topped with 3 tablespoons *bacon-flavored salad dressing or green goddess salad dressing.* Serves 4.

zucchini and cheese

Prepare one 10-ounce package frozen *zucchini* according to package directions; drain. Cut one 3-ounce package *cream cheese* into small pieces. Stir cream cheese, 3 tablespoons chopped *walnuts,* and 1 tablespoon *milk* into zucchini. Heat till cheese melts, stirring gently. Serves 4.

tangy tarragon vegetable

Prepare one 10-ounce package frozen *asparagus spears or whole kernel corn* according to package directions; drain. Stir in 3 tablespoons *butter or margarine* till melted. Stir in ½ teaspoon *lemon juice* and ⅛ teaspoon *dried tarragon,* crushed. Makes 4 servings.

oriental vegetable

Melt 1 tablespoon *butter.* Stir in one 12-ounce can *fried rice* and one 8½-ounce can *honey pod peas,* drained; heat through. Serves 4.

broccoli amandine

Prepare one 10-ounce package frozen *broccoli spears* according to package directions; drain. Melt ¼ cup *butter or margarine.* Stir in ¼ cup *slivered blanched almonds;* cook and stir till lightly browned. Toss with hot broccoli. Serves 4.

glazed vegetable

Combine 2 tablespoons *brown sugar,* 2 tablespoons *orange juice,* and 1 tablespoon *butter or margarine.* Cook and stir till sugar dissolves. Stir in one 16-ounce can *sliced beets or sliced carrots,* drained; heat through. Serves 3 or 4.

honey-raisin sweet potatoes

Combine one 9-ounce can small whole *sweet potatoes,* drained; 2 tablespoons *raisins;* 2 tablespoons *honey;* and few dashes ground *nutmeg.* Heat through. Serves 2.

vegetables

spinach-potato combo

Total time: 20 minutes

   **1 10-ounce package frozen
      chopped spinach**
   ¼ cup water
   1 teaspoon salt
   1⅓ cups water
   ⅔ cup milk
   **3 tablespoons butter *or*
      margarine**
   ½ teaspoon salt
   **1⅓ cups packaged instant
      mashed potato buds**
   **2 tablespoons cooked
      bacon pieces**
   **3 ounces shredded
      cheese (¾ cup)**

In a saucepan combine spinach, ¼ cup water, and 1 teaspoon salt. Cook, covered, 10 minutes or till tender. Drain well. Meanwhile, in a saucepan combine 1⅓ cups water, the milk, butter or margarine, and the ½ teaspoon salt. Bring to boiling; remove from heat. Stir in potato buds. Stir together cooked spinach, potato mixture, and bacon pieces; turn into 1-quart casserole. Sprinkle with cheese. Place under broiler for 1 to 2 minutes or till cheese melts. Makes 6 servings.

saucy potatoes

Total time: 15 minutes

   **1 11-ounce can condensed
      cheddar cheese soup**
   ½ cup dairy sour cream
   **1 teaspoon minced dried
      onion**
   **2 16-ounce cans sliced
      potatoes, drained**
   **½ teaspoon dried parsley
      flakes**

Combine soup and sour cream. Stir in dried onion and dash *pepper;* stir in potatoes. Cook about 7 minutes or till heated through, stirring occasionally (do not boil). Sprinkle with parsley. Serves 6.

creamy brussels sprouts

Total time: 30 minutes

   **1 10-ounce package frozen
      brussels sprouts**
   **1 10¾-ounce can
      condensed cream of
      potato soup**
   ½ teaspoon dried dillweed
   ⅓ cup crushed potato chips

Prepare brussels sprouts according to package directions; drain. Stir in soup, dillweed, and ¼ cup *water;* heat through. Turn into a 1-quart casserole; sprinkle chips atop. Bake in 375° oven about 15 minutes. Serves 4.

green beans in cream

Assembling time: 15 minutes
Cooking time: 10 minutes

   **1 9-ounce package frozen
      cut green beans**
   **1 4-ounce can sliced
      mushrooms, drained**
   **2 tablespoons chopped
      green onion**
   ¼ cup water
   **½ cup whipping cream *or*
      light cream**
   1 teaspoon cornstarch

Run hot water over frozen beans in colander till partially thawed; break vegetables apart with a fork. In saucepan combine beans, mushrooms, and green onion. Stir in ¼ cup water. Bring to boiling; reduce heat. Cover and simmer 5 minutes; drain. Stir together whipping cream or light cream and cornstarch; add to cooked beans. Cook and stir till thickened and bubbly. Cook and stir 1 to 2 minutes more. Season with salt and pepper. Makes 4 servings.

salads

layered vegetable salad

Assembling time: 20 minutes
Chilling time: 24 hours

- 1 10-ounce package frozen cauliflower
- 1 medium head lettuce, torn
- 1 4-ounce package (1 cup) shredded sharp cheddar cheese
- 1 4-ounce container whipped cream cheese with blue cheese
- ¼ cup Italian salad dressing
- 2 tablespoons sliced green onion *or* cooked bacon pieces

Run hot water over frozen cauliflower in colander till thawed; drain. Halve any large pieces of cauliflower. In bottom of large glass bowl place *half* the torn lettuce; sprinkle with salt and pepper. Arrange thawed cauliflower atop lettuce; place cheddar cheese atop cauliflower. Top with remaining lettuce. Beat together cream cheese and salad dressing. Spread over top, sealing to edge of bowl. Cover tightly and refrigerate up to 24 hours.

Garnish salad with sliced green onion or bacon chips. Toss salad before serving. Makes 8 servings.

dilled potato salad

Assembling time: 15 minutes

- ⅔ cup dairy sour cream
- 1 tablespoon milk
- 2 teaspoons vinegar
- 1 teaspoon sugar
- 1 teaspoon minced dried onion
- ½ teaspoon salt
- ½ teaspoon dried dillweed
- ¼ teaspoon pepper
- 1 29-ounce can whole new potatoes, chilled and drained
- 10 radishes, sliced

In a medium bowl stir together the sour cream, milk, vinegar, sugar, minced dried onion, salt, dried dillweed, and the pepper.

Halve the chilled potatoes (quarter any large potatoes); place in a bowl. Add the radish slices: Gently stir in the sour cream mixture. Makes 4 servings.

marinated bean salad

Assembling time: 20 minutes
Chilling time: 2 hours

- 1 9-ounce package frozen cut green beans
- 1 15-ounce can garbanzo beans, drained
- 1 8-ounce can red kidney beans, drained
- 1 2-ounce jar sliced pimiento, chopped and drained
- ¼ cup vinegar
- ¼ cup cooking oil
- 2 teaspoons sugar
- ½ teaspoon dry mustard
- ½ teaspoon dried basil, crushed
- ¼ teaspoon salt
- ⅛ teaspoon pepper
- 1 tablespoon cooked bacon pieces

Run hot water over frozen green beans in colander about 1 minute or till thawed; drain well. In bowl combine green beans, garbanzo beans, kidney beans, and pimiento. In saucepan combine vinegar, oil, sugar, dry mustard, basil, salt, and pepper; mix well. Heat to boiling. Pour dressing over bean mixture. Refrigerate 2 hours. Using slotted spoon, remove beans from marinade to individual lettuce-lined plates. Sprinkle with bacon pieces. Makes 8 servings.

73

salads

overnight fruit salad

Assembling time: 20 minutes
Chilling time: 4 to 24 hours

1 small head cabbage, shredded (about 5 cups)
1 15½-ounce can pineapple chunks, well drained
2 11-ounce cans mandarin orange sections, drained
2 cups seedless green grapes
⅓ cup light raisins
1½ cups cubed Edam cheese
1 8-ounce carton lemon yogurt
1 cup dairy sour cream

Place cabbage on bottom of large salad bowl. Top with pineapple chunks, mandarin orange sections, grapes, and raisins. Sprinkle cheese atop. Combine yogurt and sour cream; spread over salad, sealing to edge of bowl. Cover and refrigerate for 4 to 24 hours. If desired, garnish with a lemon and lime twist, curly endive, and a grape. Makes 6 servings.

Layer cabbage, fruit, and cheese for *Overnight Fruit Salad.* Chill up to 24 hours, toss, and serve.

shredded zucchini salad

Total time: 15 minutes

1 cup shredded zucchini
¼ cup sour cream with French onion
½ teaspoon Dijon-style mustard
4 lettuce leaves
2 medium tomatoes, sliced

Drain shredded zucchini. Combine sour cream, mustard, and zucchini. On four individual salad plates, arrange lettuce and tomato slices. Top tomato with zucchini mixture. Serves 4.

cottage-potato salad

Total time: 15 minutes

1 15-ounce can mayonnaise-style potato salad, chilled
1 cup cream-style cottage cheese with chives
6 radishes, sliced
2 tablespoons cooked bacon pieces
1 tablespoon finely chopped onion
Lettuce cups

Combine potato salad, cottage cheese, radishes, bacon pieces, and onion. Spoon into lettuce cups. Serves 6.

gingered cranberry-pear salad

Total time: 15 minutes

1 8-ounce can jellied cranberry sauce, chilled
¼ cup chopped walnuts
2 tablespoons chopped raisins
¼ teaspoon ground ginger
1 16-ounce can pear halves, chilled and drained
Leaf lettuce

Crush jellied cranberry sauce with fork. Stir in walnuts, raisins, and ginger. Fill pear halves with cranberry mixture. Serve on lettuce-lined plates. Makes 4 or 5 servings.
Note: Try serving this tangy relish over canned peaches or pineapple rings.

salads

banana-citrus salad

Total time: 10 minutes

- **1 11-ounce can mandarin orange sections, chilled and drained**
- **1 8-ounce can pineapple chunks, chilled and drained**
- **2 medium bananas, sliced**
- **⅓ cup lemon yogurt**
- **2 tablespoons mayonnaise *or* salad dressing**
- **Lettuce**
- **2 tablespoons chopped walnuts *or* pecans**

Toss together mandarin orange sections, pineapple chunks, and banana slices. Stir together lemon yogurt and mayonnaise or salad dressing; pour over fruit. Toss to coat fruit. Spoon mixture into a lettuce-lined bowl. Sprinkle with nuts. Serve immediately. Makes 5 or 6 servings.
Note: Chill fruit in cans at least 1 hour before preparing salad, or chill salad 1 hour before serving.

frozen peach salad

Assembling time: 35 minutes
Freezing time: 1½ hours

- **1 4½-ounce container frozen whipped dessert topping**
- **1 4-ounce container whipped cream cheese**
- **1 21-ounce can peach pie filling**
- **1 16-ounce can peach slices, drained**
- **Lettuce**

Let whipped dessert topping and cream cheese stand at room temperature 25 minutes; beat together. Fold in pie filling and peach slices.
Line muffin pans (10) with paper bake cups; spoon in peach mixture. Cover and freeze 1½ hours. To serve, peel off paper and serve on individual lettuce-lined plates. Makes 10 servings.
Note: Use a wire whisk to beat together the whipped dessert topping and the cream cheese.

molded carrot salad

Assembling time: 20 minutes
Chilling time: 1 hour

- **1 3-ounce package lemon-flavored gelatin**
- **½ cup boiling water**
- **2 cups ice cubes**
- **1 cup shredded carrot**
- **¼ cup raisins**
- **¼ cup chopped nuts**

In medium saucepan dissolve lemon gelatin in boiling water. Add ice cubes. Stir constantly for 3 minutes or till gelatin starts to thicken; remove any remaining ice cubes.
Fold in shredded carrot, raisins, and nuts. Spoon mixture into 6 individual molds. Chill in refrigerator 1 hour or till set. Makes 6 servings.

breads, rice, and pasta

romano sesame rolls

Pictured on pages 68 and 69

Assembling time: 10 minutes
Cooking time: 15 minutes

3 tablespoons butter *or* margarine
1 package (6) refrigerated flaky dinner rolls
2 teaspoons sesame seed
1 teaspoon dried parsley flakes
¼ teaspoon garlic powder
¼ cup grated Romano cheese

In an 8x1½-inch round baking pan melt butter or margarine in a 400° oven. Meanwhile, separate dough into 6 rolls; snip each into 6 pieces.

Spread melted butter in pan to coat bottom. Sprinkle sesame seed, parsley, and garlic powder evenly over butter. In plastic bag shake snipped rolls in cheese. Arrange snipped rolls in pan; sprinkle with any remaining cheese from bag.

Bake in 400° oven about 15 minutes or till golden. Turn out onto serving plate. Serve warm. Makes 8 servings.

two-tone cinnamon loaves

Pictured on page 78

Assembling time: 70 minutes
Cooking time: 35 minutes

1 16-ounce loaf *each* frozen whole wheat bread dough and white bread dough, thawed
½ cup sugar
2 teaspoons ground cinnamon
¼ cup butter, melted

Divide each loaf lengthwise into 4 portions; shape each into a 14-inch-long rope. Combine sugar and cinnamon; sprinkle on a 16x12-inch piece of waxed paper. Brush ropes with some melted butter, then roll in sugar mixture to coat. Twist together a whole wheat rope with a white rope. Secure ends. Place lengthwise in a greased 8x4x2-inch loaf pan. Repeat with a white and a whole wheat rope; place twist alongside twist in pan. Make two more twists; place side by side in another greased 8x4x2-inch loaf pan.

Cover; let rise in a warm place till almost double (45 minutes). Brush twists with remaining butter; bake in 350° oven 25 minutes. Cover with foil; bake 5 to 10 minutes more. Remove from pans; cool. Makes 2.

sticky pull-apart rolls

Assembling time: 80 minutes
Cooking time: 40 minutes

1 package 4-serving-size *regular* butterscotch pudding mix
1 cup chopped walnuts
½ cup packed brown sugar
¼ cup butter *or* margarine, softened
1 teaspoon ground cinnamon
2 16-ounce loaves frozen white bread dough, thawed

In mixing bowl combine pudding mix, walnuts, sugar, butter or margarine, and cinnamon. Stir till crumbly. Cut each bread loaf in half lengthwise, then into 8 pieces crosswise. (Each loaf should make 16 pieces total.)

Sprinkle ¼ of the pudding mixture into each of two greased 9x5x3-inch loaf pans. Arrange 16 dough pieces in each. Sprinkle the remaining pudding mixture over each. Cover and let rise in a warm place till almost double (about 1 hour). Bake in 350° oven for 35 to 40 minutes. Turn out of pans immediately. Serve warm. Makes 2 loaves.

77

breads, rice, and pasta

mexicali bubble loaf

Assembling time: 2 hours
Cooking time: 25 minutes

- 1 13¾-ounce package hot roll mix
- ¾ cup warm water (110° to 115°)
- 1 egg
- 2 tablespoons taco seasoning mix
- 3 tablespoons yellow cornmeal
- 2 tablespoons sesame seed
- 2 tablespoons finely chopped green pepper
- 2 tablespoons chopped pitted ripe olives
- 2 tablespoons finely chopped pimiento
- ¼ cup butter, melted

In a large mixing bowl dissolve yeast from hot roll mix in the ¾ cup warm water according to package directions; stir in the egg. In another bowl combine the flour mixture from roll mix and the taco seasoning mix; add to yeast mixture and stir till well blended. Turn dough out onto a lightly floured surface; knead 1 minute. Shape into a ball. Place in a greased bowl; turn once. Cover; let rise in warm place till double (30 to 45 minutes).

In a small bowl combine cornmeal and sesame seed; set aside. In another small bowl combine the chopped

Mexicali Bubble Loaf,
Two-Tone Cinnamon Loaves
(see recipe, page 77), and
Beer-Onion Bagels.

green pepper, ripe olives, and pimiento. Divide dough into 24 pieces; shape each into a ball. Dip each ball in the melted butter, then in the cornmeal mixture to coat. Arrange 12 balls in the bottom of a greased 6½-cup metal ring mold. Sprinkle olive mixture atop. Place remaining balls over filling. Cover; let rise in a warm place till double (about 45 minutes).

Bake in a 375° oven 15 minutes. Cover with foil to prevent over-browning; bake 5 to 10 minutes more or till golden. Immediately turn out of mold. Cool slightly; serve warm. Makes 1 loaf.

beer-onion bagels

Assembling time: 2 hours
Cooking time: 50 minutes

- 1 13¾-ounce package hot roll mix
- ¼ cup grated Parmesan cheese
- 3 tablespoons sugar
- 1 cup beer
- ½ cup finely chopped onion
- 3 tablespoons butter

In a large mixing bowl combine flour mixture from hot roll mix, the cheese, and *2 tablespoons* sugar. In a saucepan heat beer just till warm (110° to 115°); dissolve yeast from roll mix in warm beer. Stir yeast

mixture into flour mixture; stir till well blended. Turn out onto a lightly floured surface; knead 1 to 2 minutes. Shape into a ball. Place in a greased bowl; turn once. Cover; let rise in a warm place till double (45 to 60 minutes).

Divide dough into 12 portions; shape each into a smooth ball. With a floured finger, punch a hole into the center of each ball; pull dough gently around hole to make a smooth opening 1½ to 2 inches in diameter, working each into a uniform shape. Place shaped bagels on a greased baking sheet. Cover; let rise in a warm place till double (about 30 minutes).

Broil raised bagels on baking sheet 5 inches from heat for 1½ to 2 minutes. Turn bagels; broil 1½ to 2 minutes more (tops should not brown). In a large kettle or Dutch oven combine the remaining 1 tablespoon sugar with 1 gallon *water.* Bring to boiling; reduce heat. Cook 4 or 5 bagels at a time for 7 minutes, turning once; drain on paper toweling. Meanwhile, in small skillet cook onion in butter till tender but not brown; set aside. Place drained bagels on well greased baking sheet. Bake in 375° oven for 10 minutes. Brush or spoon onion mixture atop bagels; bake 15 to 20 minutes more or till tops are golden brown. Makes 12.

breads, rice, and pasta

refrig-a-rise rye bread

Pictured on page 13

Assembling time: 45 minutes
Chilling time: 2 to 24 hours
Cooking time: 45 minutes

3¼ to 3¾ cups all-purpose
    flour
1 package active dry yeast
2 teaspoons caraway seed
2 cups warm water
    (115° to 120°)
¼ cup molasses
1 tablespoon cooking oil
1 teaspoon salt
2½ cups rye flour
1 beaten egg white

Combine *2½ cups* of the all-purpose flour, the yeast, and *1 teaspoon* caraway seed. Mix water, molasses, oil, and salt; add to flour mixture. Beat at low speed of electric mixer ½ minute, scraping bowl. Beat 3 minutes at high speed. Stir in rye flour and as much of the remaining all-purpose flour as you can with a spoon. Turn onto floured surface. Knead in enough remaining flour to make a moderately stiff dough that is smooth and elastic (6 to 8 minutes). Halve dough. Cover with plastic wrap and a towel; let rest 20 minutes.

    Shape loaves. Place in two greased 8x4x2-inch loaf pans. Brush with more oil. Cover loosely with plastic wrap. Refrigerate 2 to 24 hours.

Before baking, let stand, uncovered, at room temperature 10 minutes. Prick any bubbles. Brush loaves with egg white; sprinkle remaining 1 teaspoon caraway seed atop. Bake in 350° oven 45 minutes; cover with foil last 10 minutes. Remove; cool. Makes 2 loaves.

refrig-a-rise dinner rolls

Variation pictured on pages 68 and 69

Assembling time: 80 minutes
Chilling time: 2 to 24 hours
Cooking time: 25 minutes

4½ to 5 cups all-purpose
    flour
1 package active dry yeast
1 cup milk
½ cup sugar
½ cup butter *or* margarine
1 teaspoon salt
3 eggs
    Butter *or* margarine,
    melted

In large mixer bowl combine *2 cups* of the flour and the yeast. In saucepan heat milk, sugar, the ½ cup butter or margarine, and salt just till warm (115° to 120°), stirring constantly. Add to dry mixture in mixer bowl; add eggs. Beat at low speed of electric mixer for ½ minute, scraping bowl. Beat 3 minutes at high speed. Stir in as much of the remain-

ing flour as you can with a spoon. Turn out onto a lightly floured surface; knead in enough remaining flour to make a moderately stiff dough that is smooth and elastic (6 to 8 minutes). Halve dough. Shape into balls, cover, and let rest 20 minutes.

    Punch down. Shape each half into 16 rolls. Place rolls in two lightly greased 8x8x2-inch baking pans. Brush rolls lightly with melted butter. Cover with oiled waxed paper, then with clear plastic wrap. Refrigerate 2 to 24 hours. When ready to bake, remove rolls from refrigerator, uncover, and let stand 20 minutes.

    Just before baking, puncture any surface bubbles using a greased wooden pick. Bake in 375° oven for 20 to 25 minutes. Remove from pans. Serve warm. Makes 32 rolls.

Orange Rolls
Prepare and bake Refrig-a-Rise Dinner Rolls as directed above. Meanwhile, for orange glaze, in saucepan combine ⅓ cup *sugar* and 1 tablespoon *cornstarch*. Stir in ⅓ cup *frozen orange juice concentrate* (thawed) and 2 tablespoons *butter or margarine*. Cook and stir till thickened and bubbly. Cook and stir 1 to 2 minutes more; set aside to cool.

    Remove baked rolls from pans to wire racks. Place waxed paper under racks to catch glaze drippings, then brush hot rolls with orange glaze. Serve warm.

curried risotto

Pictured on page 35

Assembling time: 5 minutes
Cooking time: 25 minutes

3 cups water
1 cup long grain rice
2 tablespoons butter *or*
    margarine
1 tablespoon instant
    chicken bouillon
    granules
1 teaspoon minced dried
    onion
1 teaspoon curry powder
    Dash pepper
½ cup light raisins
⅓ cup peanuts
    Parsley

In saucepan combine water, rice, butter or margarine, bouillon granules, dried onion, curry powder, and pepper. Bring to a rolling boil; reduce heat to low. Cover with a tight-fitting lid. Continue cooking for 15 minutes (do not lift cover). Remove from heat. Let stand, covered, for 5 to 8 minutes. Stir in raisins and peanuts.

To serve, garnish with a sprig of parsley. Makes 6 servings.

pasta primavera

Pictured on pages 68 and 69

Total time: 40 minutes

4 ounces linguine
¼ cup butter *or* margarine
1 cup thinly sliced fresh
    broccoli
1 medium carrot, thinly
    sliced
½ cup sliced green onion
1 clove garlic, minced
1 teaspoon dried basil,
    crushed
½ teaspoon salt
¼ teaspoon pepper
1½ cups sliced fresh
    mushrooms
1 6-ounce package frozen
    pea pods
¼ cup dry white wine
    Grated Parmesan cheese

Cook linguine in boiling salted water till tender; drain and keep warm.

Meanwhile, melt butter or margarine in 10-inch skillet. Stir in broccoli, carrot, onion, garlic, basil, salt, and pepper. Cook for 6 to 7 minutes or till broccoli is just tender. Add mushrooms; cook about 2 minutes or till tender. Add pea pods and wine. Cover and cook 2 minutes or till vegetables are crisp-tender. Stir in linguine; toss. Turn mixture into serving bowl. Sprinkle Parmesan cheese atop and toss. Makes 4 servings.

fried spaghetti

Assembling time: 15 minutes
Cooking time: 10 minutes

5 ounces spaghetti
2 eggs
½ of a 4-ounce package
    (½ cup) shredded
    mozzarella cheese
¼ cup grated Parmesan
    cheese
1 teaspoon minced dried
    onion
½ teaspoon dried basil,
    crushed
¼ teaspoon salt
    Dash pepper
2 tablespoons butter *or*
    margarine

Cook spaghetti according to package directions; drain. Meanwhile, beat together eggs, mozzarella cheese, Parmesan cheese, dried onion, basil, salt, and pepper. Pour egg mixture over spaghetti; toss to coat.

Melt butter or margarine in a 10-inch skillet. Add the spaghetti mixture. Cook without stirring over medium heat about 10 minutes or till bottom is golden. To serve, turn out of skillet onto serving plate, browned side up. Cut into wedges. Makes 6 servings.
Note: You can substitute 2½ cups leftover cooked spaghetti for the uncooked spaghetti.

fast-and-easy
DESSERTS

Enjoy desserts every day! You'll find tasty yet effortless recipes in this chapter. These include elegant desserts for entertaining, quick snacks, and simple desserts for everyday meals.

Choose from recipes that can be made and stored in the refrigerator or freezer till serving time. Or, prepare a parfait, fruit, or candy recipe to serve promptly. Need a last-minute dessert? Turn to *Quick Dessert Fix-Ups* for surprisingly simple treats.

Pictured: *Orange Yogurt Short-cake* (see recipe, page 84) uses a sugar cookie mix to shortcut the traditional cake recipe and has a fluffy filling of yogurt and cream cheese. *Peach Almond Ice Cream* (see recipe, page 88) is a simple combination of buttermilk, peach preserves, and almond extract that's frozen, whipped, and refrozen. Top each serving with almonds for a refreshing dessert.

coconut spice pudding cakes

Assembling time: 15 minutes
Cooking time: 25 minutes

**1 package 1-layer-size spice
    cake mix**
**1 package 4-serving-size
    regular coconut cream
    pudding mix**

Grease and lightly flour eight
6-ounce custard cups. Prepare
cake mix according to package directions. Turn batter into
custard cups. Stir together
pudding mix and 2¼ cups
water; pour over cake batter.
Bake in 350° oven 20 to 25
minutes. Serve warm. Serves 8.

pumpkin nut cake

Total time: 35 minutes

**1 package 1-layer-size
    white cake mix**
1 egg
½ cup canned pumpkin
**½ teaspoon ground
    cinnamon**
¼ teaspoon ground nutmeg
⅓ cup chopped nuts

Stir together the first five ingredients and ¼ cup *water*.
Beat on medium speed of
electric mixer 2 minutes. Turn

into a greased 8x8x2-inch baking pan. Top with nuts. Bake
in 350° oven 20 to 25 minutes.
Cool. Serves 9.

pineapple-cinnamon shortcakes

Total time: 35 minutes

¼ cup sugar
**1 teaspoon ground
    cinnamon**
**1 package (6) refrigerated
    flaky dinner rolls**
**2 tablespoons butter *or*
    margarine, melted**
**1 15½-ounce can crushed
    pineapple, drained**
**Pressurized dessert
    topping**

In bowl combine sugar and
cinnamon. Separate dough
into 6 rolls. Dip tops and sides
in butter or margarine, then in
sugar-cinnamon mixture. Bake
according to package directions till lightly browned. Cool
slightly; split rolls in half.
Spoon about ¾ of the pineapple over the bottom portion of
the rolls; cover each with
some dessert topping. Place
top portion of rolls atop fruit
and dessert topping. Spoon
the remaining pineapple over
rolls. Top each with some dessert topping. Serve immediately. Makes 6 servings.

orange yogurt shortcake

Pictured on pages 82 and 83

Assembling time: 10 minutes
Cooking time: 25 minutes
Before serving: 15 minutes

2 beaten eggs
½ cup milk
½ teaspoon orange extract
**1 package 3-dozen-size
    sugar cookie mix**
**1 8-ounce package cream
    cheese, cubed**
¾ cup orange yogurt
**2 tablespoons powdered
    sugar**
**1 11-ounce can mandarin
    orange sections,
    drained**

Combine eggs, milk, and extract; stir in cookie mix.
Spread batter in 2 greased
and floured 8x1½-inch round
baking pans. Bake in 350°
oven for 20 to 25 minutes.
Cool 10 minutes; remove from
pans. Cool.
    Beat cream cheese till fluffy.
Add yogurt and sugar. Beat at
low speed of electric mixer
just till combined. Spread *half*
of the yogurt mixture on top
surface of one cake layer. Arrange about ⅔ of the orange
sections atop. Place second
cake layer atop. Spread remaining yogurt mixture over
cake. Arrange remaining
orange sections atop. Garnish
with lemon leaves, if desired.
Serve immediately. Serves 10.

apple-oatmeal coffee cake

Assembling time: 25 minutes
Cooking time: 35 minutes

1 package 3-dozen-size oatmeal cookie mix
¼ cup chopped walnuts
2 tablespoons butter *or* margarine, melted
½ teaspoon ground cinnamon
2 beaten eggs
⅓ cup milk
1 cup coarsely chopped, peeled apple

For topping, measure ½ *cup* of the cookie mix into a small bowl; stir in walnuts, butter or margarine, and cinnamon. Set aside. In mixing bowl combine the remaining cookie mix, eggs, and milk. Fold in chopped apple. Spread batter in a greased 9x9x2-inch baking pan. Sprinkle reserved topping evenly over batter. Bake in 350° oven about 35 minutes or till done. To serve, cut into squares and serve warm. Makes 9 servings.

java-rum torte

Assembling time: 35 minutes
Chilling time: 1 hour

½ cup sugar
½ cup water
2 tablespoons instant coffee crystals
2 tablespoons rum
1 tablespoon butter *or* margarine
1 10¾-ounce frozen loaf pound cake, thawed
1 1½-ounce envelope dessert topping mix, whipped

In 1½-quart saucepan combine sugar, water, and coffee crystals. Bring to full rolling boil; boil 3 minutes over medium heat, stirring occasionally to prevent boiling over. Remove from heat; stir in rum and butter or margarine. Cool 5 minutes. Slice cake lengthwise into 3 layers. Spoon *3 tablespoons* of coffee mixture over bottom layer; spread with ⅓ of the whipped topping. Stack middle layer atop bottom layer; repeat topping with coffee mixture and whipped topping. Spoon *3 tablespoons* coffee mixture atop *cut surface* of top layer; invert and place atop stack. Spread remaining whipped topping over top. Bring remaining coffee mixture to a rolling boil; boil 1 minute, stirring constantly. Cool 10 minutes. Drizzle atop torte. Chill torte 1 hour or till serving time. Serves 8.

shortcut flan

Assembling time: 10 minutes
Baking time: 50 minutes
Chilling time: 1 hour

¼ cup caramel topping
4 beaten eggs
2 13-ounce cans (3½ cups) evaporated milk
½ cup sugar
2 teaspoons vanilla

Pour the caramel topping into the bottom of an 8-inch flan pan or 8x1½-inch round baking pan. Lift and tilt the pan to evenly coat the bottom. Set pan in a larger baking pan; place on oven rack.

In bowl combine the beaten eggs, evaporated milk, the sugar, and vanilla. Pour carefully into the caramel-coated pan. Add boiling water to the outer pan to depth of 1 inch. Bake in 325° oven for 45 to 50 minutes or till a knife inserted just off-center comes out clean. *Center will be soft.* Chill thoroughly. Loosen the sides of the flan. Then invert onto serving platter just before serving. Cut into wedges or spoon into dessert dishes. Makes 8 servings.

quick dessert fix-ups

applesauce fluff

Combine I cup chunk-style *applesauce* with raspberries; *1 cup frozen whipped dessert topping*, thawed; and ¼ cup toasted slivered *almonds*. Chill.Spoon over *angel cake slices*. Makes 2 cups.

brittle topping

Beat 1 cup *whipping cream* and 1 teaspoon *vanilla* till soft peaks form. Fold in ¾ cup finely crushed *peanut brittle*. Serve immediately or chill up to 2 hours. Spoon over *cake slices*. Sprinkle crushed *peanut brittle* atop. Serves 6.

cran-citrus sauce

Combine one 14-ounce can *sweetened condensed milk*, ½ cup *cranberry-orange relish*, ½ cup *water*, 2 teaspoons shredded *lemon peel*, and 2 tablespoons *lemon juice*; beat well. Chill 2 hours. Serve over *ice cream*. Makes 2¼ cups.

pudding sauce

Combine one 5-ounce can *chocolate pudding*, ¼ cup *plain yogurt*, 1 tablespoon *milk*, and few drops *almond extract*. Spoon over *angel cake slices*. Top with slivered *almonds*. Makes ¾ cup.

cherry nut sauce

In saucepan heat one 10-ounce package frozen *dark sweet cherries* till thawed. Stir in ¼ cup broken *walnuts*, 1 teaspoon *cornstarch*, and ¼ teaspoon *ground nutmeg*. Cook and stir till thickened and bubbly. Cook and stir 1 to 2 minutes more. Serve over *cake slices*. Makes 1½ cups.

sour cream-fruit sauce

Combine 1 cup *dairy sour cream*, 2 tablespoons *brown sugar*, and ¼ teaspoon *ground nutmeg*. Stir in 2 cups desired *fruit* (use 2 or more of the following fruits: pineapple chunks, blueberries, strawberries, sliced peaches, sliced bananas, or halved seedless green grapes). Serve over *cake slices* or spoon into individual *tart shells*. Serves 8.

apricot-nut sauce

Drain one 8¾-ounce can *fruit cocktail* (chilled), reserving 3 tablespoons syrup. Combine fruit cocktail, reserved syrup, one 21-ounce can *apricot pie filling* (chilled), ¼ cup broken *pecans*, and few drops *almond extract*. Slice 1 small *banana* and fold into apricot mixture. Serve over *cake slices*. Makes 3⅓ cups.

chocolate-peanut topping

Melt ½ cup *semi-sweet chocolate pieces* and 1 tablespoon *butter* over low heat, stirring occasionally. Stir in 2 tablespoons *milk*. To serve, spoon hot sauce over servings of *vanilla ice cream*. Top with shredded *coconut* and chopped *peanuts*. Serves 4.

double fruit sauce

Drain one 8¾-ounce can *peach slices* or one 8½-ounce can *pear slices*, reserving 2 tablespoons syrup. In saucepan heat ¼ cup *plum jelly* and reserved syrup till jelly is melted. Top servings of *vanilla ice cream* with peach or pear slices; drizzle warm plum jelly over each. Makes 4 servings.

pear-pecan sauce

In skillet melt 2 tablespoons *butter or margarine*. Stir in ¼ cup chopped *pecans* and 2 tablespoons *brown sugar*. Add one 16-ounce can *pear slices*, drained. Cook and stir over medium heat about 4 minutes or till heated through. Remove from heat; keep warm. Heat 3 tablespoons light *rum*; add to pears. Ignite. When flame subsides, spoon mixture over *vanilla ice cream*. Serves 4 to 6.

chocolate fondue

Total time: 20 minutes

⅓ cup evaporated milk
1 package creamy
   chocolate frosting mix
   (for 2-layer cake)
2 tablespoons butter
   Apple chunks, cake
   cubes, *or* banana slices
¾ cup chopped pecans

Blend milk into frosting mix, stirring till smooth. Add butter. Cook and stir till butter is melted. To serve, transfer to fondue pot; keep warm over fondue burner. Dip fruit into sauce, then into nuts. If necessary, thin mixture with additional milk. Serves 6.

cheesy peaches

Total time: 10 minutes

1 29-ounce can peach
   halves, chilled
   (6 halves)
1 4-ounce container
   whipped cream cheese
2 tablespoons powdered
   sugar
¼ teaspoon ground nutmeg

Drain peaches, reserving 1 teaspoon syrup. Combine reserved peach syrup, cream cheese, sugar, and nutmeg; beat till fluffy. Spoon into each peach half. Serves 6.

strawberry cheesecake pie

Assembling time: 20 minutes
Freezing time: 3 hours

1 8-ounce package cream
   cheese, softened
1 14-ounce can *sweetened
   condensed* milk
1 cup frozen loose pack
   unsweetened
   strawberries, thawed
¼ cup lemon juice
1 9-inch graham cracker pie
   shell
   Frozen whipped dessert
   topping, thawed

In mixer bowl beat cream cheese till light and fluffy. Add condensed milk, strawberries, and lemon juice. Beat at low speed of electric mixer till smooth. Spoon mixture into the pie shell. Freeze 3 hours or till firm. Let stand at room temperature for 5 minutes before serving. Garnish each serving with a dollop of the whipped dessert topping. Makes 8 servings.

peanut butter-cream cheese pie

Assembling time: 25 minutes
Chilling time: 1½ hours

2 3-ounce packages cream
   cheese, softened
¾ cup sifted powdered
   sugar
½ cup peanut butter
2 tablespoons milk
1 1½-ounce envelope
   dessert topping mix
1 9-inch graham cracker pie
   shell
   Coarsely chopped
   peanuts

In small mixer bowl beat together softened cream cheese and powdered sugar till light and fluffy. Add peanut butter and milk, beating till mixture is smooth and creamy. Prepare the dessert topping mix according to package directions; fold into peanut butter-cream cheese mixture. Turn mixture into pie shell. Chill at least 1½ hours or till serving time. Garnish top of pie with the chopped peanuts. Makes 8 servings.

chilly cappuccino pie

Assembling time: 25 minutes
Freezing time: 4 hours

 1 pint vanilla ice cream, cut
    into ½-inch slices
 1 purchased chocolate
    wafer pie shell
 3 tablespoons instant
    Italian-style coffee
    powder *or* 2 teaspoons
    instant coffee crystals
 1 cup milk
 1 cup dairy sour cream
 ⅛ teaspoon ground nutmeg
 1 package 4-serving-size
    instant chocolate
    pudding mix
    Frozen whipped dessert
    topping, thawed
    Chocolate curls

Arrange ice cream slices on
bottom of wafer pie shell. If
necessary, spread ice cream
using back of spoon to cover
bottom of shell. Smooth top;
return to freezer. Meanwhile,
in small mixer bowl dissolve
coffee powder or coffee crystals in milk. Add sour cream
and nutmeg; beat with electric
mixer till smooth. Add pudding
mix; beat till smooth and thickened. Spread evenly over ice
cream, swirling top to form de-
sign. Freeze 4 to 6 hours or
overnight. Garnish with dollops
of dessert topping and chocolate curls. Makes 8 servings.

peach almond ice cream

Pictured on pages 82 and 83

Assembling time: 10 minutes
Freezing time: 5 hours

 2 cups buttermilk
 1 cup peach preserves
    Few drops almond extract

Stir buttermilk into preserves;
stir in extract. Pour into 8x8x2-
inch pan; freeze firm. Break up
frozen mixture; place into
chilled mixer bowl. Beat with
electric mixer till fluffy. Return
to pan. Cover; freeze firm
(about 2½ hours). If desired,
garnish servings with sliced almonds and mint leaves.
Makes about 1 quart.

crunchy parfaits

Total time: 15 minutes

 1 16-ounce can red
    raspberries, chilled, *or*
    one 15-ounce can
    blueberries, chilled
 1 8-ounce carton lemon
    yogurt
 ¾ cup granola with coconut
    and honey

Drain fruit; divide *half* of the
fruit among 4 parfait glasses.
Dollop *half* the yogurt over the
fruit. Sprinkle *half* the granola
atop. Repeat layering. Chill till
serving time. Serves 4.

tropical lemon chiffon parfaits

Total time: 40 minutes

 1 8-ounce can crushed
    pineapple (juice pack)
 ½ cup water
 1 3-ounce package lemon-
    flavored gelatin
 2½ cups ice cubes
    (about 10)
 1 9-ounce container frozen
    whipped dessert
    topping, thawed
 1¼ cups crumbled coconut
    macaroons
    Toasted coconut
    (optional)

Drain pineapple, reserving
juice (about ½ cup). Set pineapple aside. In saucepan combine reserved juice and water;
bring to boiling. Remove from
heat. Add gelatin; stir till dissolved. Add ice cubes and stir
about 2 minutes or till gelatin
is thickened. Remove any un-
melted ice. Stir in thawed dessert topping; beat till smooth.
Fold in pineapple. Chill, if necessary, till mixture mounds
with spoon. Spoon mixture into
parfait glasses, alternating
with crumbled macaroons.
Chill. If desired, garnish with
toasted coconut. Makes 10
servings.

**Try these cool dessert
delights—***Chilly Cappuccino
Pie* and *Tropical Lemon
Chiffon Parfaits.*

pineapple-coconut dessert

Total time: 15 minutes

- 1 1½-ounce envelope dessert topping mix
- 1½ cups cold milk
- 2 tablespoons light rum
- 1 package 4-serving-size *instant* pineapple cream *or* vanilla pudding mix
- ¾ cup coconut
- 1 8¼-ounce can crushed pineapple, drained
  Toasted coconut (optional)

In large mixer bowl prepare dessert topping mix according to package directions except use *½ cup* of the cold milk and the light rum instead of the liquid called for. Add the pudding mix and remaining *1 cup* milk. Blend together. Beat at high speed of electric mixer for 2 minutes. Stir in ¾ cup coconut. Scoop mixture into sherbet or parfait dishes. Chill till serving time. To serve, top with crushed pineapple. Sprinkle toasted coconut atop, if desired. Makes 6 servings.

frozen cherry-almond molds

Assembling time: 20 minutes
Freezing time: 3 hours

- 1 pint vanilla ice cream
- 1 21-ounce can cherry pie filling
- 2 tablespoons Amaretto
- ½ cup chopped almonds *or* pecans

Let ice cream stand at room temperature 10 minutes to soften. Combine ice cream, pie filling, and Amaretto. Stir in nuts. Turn into eight 6-ounce custard cups. Freeze till firm (about 3 hours). To serve, let stand at room temperature 5 minutes, loosen with spatula. Serves 8.

fruited waffles

Total time: 15 minutes

- 1 10-ounce package frozen red raspberries *or* sliced strawberries
- 4 frozen waffles
- 1 3-ounce package cream cheese, softened

Heat frozen berries till warm. Heat waffles according to package directions. Spread ¼ of the cream cheese on each waffle. Spoon warm berries and their juice atop. Serves 4.

raspberry ice cream parfaits

Assembling time: 15 minutes
Freezing time: 10 minutes

- ¾ cup boiling water
- 1 3-ounce package raspberry-, cherry-, *or* peach-flavored gelatin
- 1 10-ounce package frozen red raspberries *or* peach slices
- 1 cup vanilla ice cream

In blender container combine boiling water and gelatin. Cover and blend at high speed about 20 seconds or till gelatin is dissolved. Cut package of frozen fruit in half; set aside half to thaw for garnish. Add remaining fruit to gelatin; cover and blend till nearly smooth. Add ice cream, a spoonful at a time, blending after each addition till smooth. Pour mixture into 4 parfait glasses; chill in freezer at least 10 minutes. Drain reserved fruit. To serve, garnish each serving with remaining fruit. Makes 4 servings.

peach-on-peach compote

Total time: 20 minutes

2 10-ounce packages frozen peach slices, thawed and drained
1 pint vanilla ice cream
1 8-ounce carton peach yogurt

Spoon peach slices into large compote or individual sherbets. Stir ice cream to soften; fold into yogurt. Spoon ice cream mixture over peaches. Serves 8.

almond cream fruit

Total time: 15 minutes

½ cup whipping cream
1 tablespoon powdered sugar
1 tablespoon Amaretto
1 16-ounce can orange and grapefruit sections, chilled

Combine whipping cream, sugar, and Amaretto; beat till soft peaks form. Drain fruit, reserving liquid. Serve fruit in individual serving dishes, spooning *1 tablespoon* reserved liquid over each. Top with whipped cream. Serves 4.

honey sugar cookies

Assembling time: 15 minutes
Cooking time: 20 minutes

1 package 3-dozen-size sugar cookie mix
2 tablespoons honey
1 teaspoon finely shredded orange peel
¾ cup granola with coconut and honey

Prepare cookie mix according to package directions. Stir in the honey and shredded orange peel. Stir in granola. Drop cookie batter from a rounded teaspoon 2 inches apart onto an ungreased cookie sheet.

Bake in 350° oven about 10 minutes or till done. Cool 1 minute. Remove from cookie sheet; cool thoroughly on wire rack. Makes about 36.

champagne fruit

Total time: 15 minutes

1 10-ounce package frozen mixed fruit
½ cup champagne *or* ginger ale, chilled
1 teaspoon lemon juice

Place unopened pouch of fruit in large bowl of warm water and let stand for 10 minutes, turning occasionally. Turn fruit into serving bowl. Combine champagne or ginger ale and lemon juice; pour over fruit. Makes 4 servings.

granola apple crisp

Assembling time: 10 minutes
Cooking time: 20 minutes

1 20-ounce can sliced apples
1 to 2 tablespoons honey
½ teaspoon ground cinnamon
¾ cup granola
2 tablespoons butter *or* margarine

In a 1-quart casserole stir together *undrained* apple slices, honey, and cinnamon. Sprinkle granola atop; dot with butter or margarine. Bake in 375° oven about 20 minutes or till heated through. Makes 4 or 5 servings.

91

easy walnut toffee

Assembling time: 35 minutes
Chilling time: 45 minutes

½ **cup butter** *or* **margarine**
¾ **cup packed brown sugar**
½ **cup semisweet chocolate**
   pieces
½ **cup chopped walnuts**

In a 1½-quart saucepan melt butter or margarine. Add brown sugar. Cook over medium heat to soft crack stage or till candy thermometer registers 290°, stirring often. Remove from heat and spread mixture into a buttered 8x8x2-inch baking pan. Let stand 3 minutes to firm surface. Sprinkle chocolate pieces atop. Let stand 1 to 2 minutes.

When chocolate is softened, spread evenly over toffee; sprinkle walnuts atop. Chill thoroughly (about 45 minutes). To serve, break into pieces. Makes about 1 pound.
Note: Test for soft-crack stage by dropping a little syrup into very cold water. Syrup should separate into threads that are not brittle.

cinnamon granola drops

Total time: 25 minutes

2 **cups sugar**
¼ **cup unsweetened cocoa**
   powder
½ **teaspoon ground**
   cinnamon
½ **cup milk**
½ **cup butter** *or* **margarine**
1 **tablespoon light corn**
   syrup
¼ **cup peanut butter**
2 **cups granola**

In heavy 3-quart saucepan combine sugar, cocoa powder, and cinnamon. Stir in milk. Add butter or margarine and corn syrup. Bring to boiling, stirring occasionally. Boil vigorously for 3 minutes, stirring occasionally. Remove from heat. Blend in peanut butter. Stir in granola.

Return mixture to boiling. Remove from heat; beat for 6 to 7 minutes or till slightly thickened. Immediately drop from a teaspoon onto waxed paper. (If mixture spreads too much, beat a little longer.) Cool. Makes about 36.
Raisin Granola Drops
Prepare Cinnamon Granola Drops as directed above *except* use ¼ teaspoon *ground cloves* instead of the ground cinnamon, and add ¼ cup *raisins* with the granola. Continue as directed above.

spiced dessert coffee

Total time: 15 minutes

6 **cups water**
½ **cup ground coffee**
6 **inches stick cinnamon,**
   broken up
8 **whole cloves**
3 **whole cardamom pods,**
   husks removed
   Frozen whipped dessert
   topping, thawed, *or*
   vanilla ice cream

Pour water into percolator; stand the stem and basket firmly in pot. Measure coffee, cinnamon, cloves, and cardamom into basket. Replace basket lid; cover pot. Bring water to boiling; reduce heat and perk gently for 5 to 8 minutes. (Or, follow manufacturer's directions for electric coffee makers.) Spoon dessert topping or ice cream atop each serving. Makes 8 six-ounce servings.
Note: For best results, perk coffee in a clean coffee maker using cold water.

index

Shortcut Tips